Comptroller of the Currency
Administrator of National Banks

Retail Lending
Examination Procedures

Comptroller's Handbook

December 2004

Assets

Retail Lending   Table of Contents

Introduction

The "Retail Lending Examination Procedures" are structured to accommodate ongoing supervision of all types of retail lending products and operations, and more comprehensive examinations of high-risk operations or larger, more complex operations. Examiners have the flexibility to add or delete procedures based on the characteristics of a bank's retail lending activities and the identified risks or areas of concern.

Minimum Examination Procedures[1]

The minimum procedures are designed to enable examiners to assess the bank's exposure to retail credit risk and to identify significant changes in the bank's performance, products, or markets during supervisory activities. The procedures provide the steps necessary for a comprehensive retail lending examination in small or less complex operations. They also serve as the base retail lending procedures for larger more complex operations.

Depending on the size, complexity, and risk profile of the retail portfolio, the minimum procedures may provide sufficient information to reach conclusions. They may also indicate the need for a more extensive review of all or parts of a bank's retail lending activities (e.g., significant changes, growth, deteriorating performance, higher-risk products, or complex operations). If more in-depth procedures are warranted, examiners should employ some or all of the supplemental procedures.

Supplemental Examination Procedures

The supplemental procedures for retail credit, which include product-specific procedures and more testing, are organized by functional and product-specific areas. These areas are:

- Management planning.
- Marketing and product development.
- Underwriting.
- Account management.

---

[1] The minimum procedures focus solely on retail credit activities. These procedures are consistent with, but not identical to, the procedures in the "Community Bank Supervision" booklet of the *Comptroller's Handbook*.

- Collections.
- Risk management and control functions.
- Profitability.
- Third-party management.
- Debt suspension and cancellation.
- Overdraft programs.

These procedures are targeted to larger, more complex operations, as well as to smaller banks that have conditions requiring more comprehensive review.

Appendixes

The appendixes provide additional tools that examiners can use to plan and to conduct retail credit examinations:

- **Transaction Testing** (appendix A) – A description of common testing used during retail lending examinations.

- **General Request Letter** (appendix B) – A sample request letter tailored for the "Minimum Examination Procedures," but also applicable to the "Supplemental Examination Procedures."

- **Uniform Retail Credit Classification and Account Management Policy Checklist** (appendix C) – An examination tool referenced in the procedures to test adherence to the requirements of OCC Bulletin 2000-20, "Uniform Retail Credit Classification and Account Management Policy."

- **Account Management and Loss Allowance Guidance Checklist** (appendix D) – An examination tool referenced in the procedures to test adherence to the requirements of OCC Bulletin 2003-1, "Account Management and Loss Allowance Guidance."

- **Debt Suspension Agreement and Debt Cancellation Contract Forms and Disclosure Worksheet** (appendix E) – An examination tool referenced in the procedures to assist in assessing compliance with 12 CFR 37 disclosure requirements.

- **Debt Suspension and Cancellation Product Information Worksheet** (appendix F) – An examination tool referenced in the procedures to assist in documenting a bank's debt suspension and cancellation practices and product characteristics.

- **Loss Forecasting Tools** (appendix G) – A description of roll rate forecasting and other forecasting techniques.

Minimum Examination Procedures

Objective: Assess the level of credit risk, evaluate the quality of risk management, and determine the aggregate level and direction of risk of the bank's retail credit activities.

The scope of retail lending supervisory activities, in aggregate or for a specific product or function, depends on the examiner's knowledge of those activities, the amount of total and product exposure, and the amount of risk posed to the bank's earnings and capital. The minimum procedures provide the steps necessary for a comprehensive retail lending examination in smaller or less complex operations, and serve as the base retail lending procedures for larger or more complex operations. The procedures include in-depth portfolio analysis and testing to promote examiners' assessments of the quantity, aggregate level, and direction of credit risk.

Expanding the scope of the review may be necessary in cases in which the bank offers new or significantly changed products, a particular concern exists, or in larger, more complex operations. In these situations, examiners should select the appropriate "Supplemental Examination Procedures" to augment the minimum procedures. The supplemental procedures are grouped by functional and product-specific areas. Examiners are also encouraged to refer to other *Comptroller's Handbook* sections, including Community and Large Bank Supervision, Allowance for Loan and Lease Losses, Concentration of Credits, Credit Card Lending, Internal and External Audits, Internal Control, Lease Financing, Loan Portfolio Management, Merchant Processing, Mortgage Banking, and Rating Credit Risk.

While reviewing retail credit activities, examiners should remain alert for lending practices and product terms that could indicate discriminatory, unfair, deceptive, abusive, or predatory issues.

Note: If the National Credit Tool (NCT) is available, examiners are encouraged to use the standard retail reports and other NCT capabilities (i.e., custom reports and sampling) to assist in the retail credit review.

1.   Review the scope, conclusions, and work papers from previous supervisory activities. Determine the adequacy and timeliness of management's response to the issues identified, and any findings or issues requiring follow-up.

---

2. Review relevant reports issued by internal and external audit, quality assurance, loan review, risk management, and compliance management since the prior supervisory activity. Determine the adequacy and timeliness of management's responses to the issues identified, and any findings or issues requiring follow-up. Request work papers, if warranted.

3. Review the minutes of retail credit-related committee meetings conducted since the prior supervisory activity.

4. Obtain copies of the OCC (complaints reported to the Customer Assistance Group) and bank consumer complaint logs and evaluate the information for significant issues and trends. *Note: Complaints serve as a valuable early warning indicator for compliance, credit, and operational issues, including discriminatory, unfair, deceptive, abusive, and predatory practices.*

5. Determine whether there is any litigation, either filed or anticipated, associated with the bank's retail credit activities and the expected cost or other implications.

6. Determine whether the bank offers debt suspension and/or cancellation (debt waiver) products. If so, ensure compliance with 12 CFR 37, Debt Cancellation Contracts and Debt Suspension Agreements, and complete the "Debt Suspension and Cancellation" section in the "Supplemental Examination Procedures," if program volume is significant.

   Note: It is important to identify debt waiver penetration and benefit activation rates early in the examination in order to fully assess retail credit portfolio performance. Accounts generally show as current while on benefits, yet portfolio analysis should recognize that these customers are not actually performing which may indicate a higher risk profile.

7. Develop an initial assessment of the quality and performance of the bank's retail credit portfolio and product segments using portfolio reports, risk management analyses, and the UBPR. Consider:
   - Growth.

- Portfolio mix and changes.
- Significance of the portfolio and each of the products in terms of total loans, total assets, and capital.
- Credit performance.
- Contribution to earnings and income composition (e.g., interest, fees).

Note: If the bank securitizes assets, also analyze data on a managed basis. Coordinate findings and conclusions with the examiner(s) assigned to review securitizations throughout the examination.

8. Discuss with management changes made since the prior supervisory activity or planned for retail credit products and operations, including:

- Growth overall and in individual products.
- Portfolio product mix.
- Off-balance-sheet retail credit activities (e.g., merchant processing, ACH payment programs, and securitization activities).
- New products.
- Terms on existing products.
- Marketing or acquisition channels (e.g., direct, mail, telemarketing, Internet, and third-party originators).
- Expansion into new market and trade areas.
- New or expanded third-party loan generation or servicing arrangements.
- Underwriting, risk selection criteria, and portfolio quality.
- Monitoring and risk management processes.
- Models used to underwrite or manage the portfolio, if any.
- Retail loan systems, including underwriting, servicing, and collection platforms.

Note: It is important to understand how management assesses the effects of changes on profitability and the risk profile, and incorporates the effects of changes into the planning and risk management processes.

Also, discuss management's perception of the competition and whether the bank can remain successful in its market without changes. Determine the extent to which the changes made or proposed were in response to the competitive environment, and the reasonableness of and analytical support for those changes.

9.   Evaluate retail credit management and the planning process. Specifically:

    (a) Determine whether retail credit objectives are consistent with the bank's strategic plan, and whether the objectives are reasonable in light of the bank's resources, expertise, product offerings, and competitive environment.

    (b) Determine whether the retail-marketing plans and budgets are consistent with the retail credit objectives and the bank's strategic plan.

    (c) Evaluate the adequacy of the retail credit planning process (growth, financial, and product-related), including the adequacy and timeliness of revisions when warranted by portfolio performance and new developments.

    (d) Determine management's risk tolerance with respect to risk and return objectives (e.g., return on assets, return on equity, or return on investment) or credit performance hurdles (e.g., delinquency, credit loss, or risk score tolerances).

    (e) Assess the qualifications, expertise, and staffing levels of management and staff in view of existing and planned retail credit activities.

10.   Review and assess the adequacy of the bank's policies, procedures, and practices. Specifically:

    (a) Determine whether consumer loan policies are approved by the board of directors at inception, and included in annual policy reviews thereafter.

    (b) Identify significant changes in underwriting criteria and terms, how credit scoring models are used, account management activities (including re-pricing and credit line management programs for open-end accounts), and collection practices and policies. Specifically:

- Determine the effect of those changes on the portfolio and its performance.

- Determine whether underwriting policies provide appropriate guidance on assessing that the borrower's capacity to repay the loan is based on a consideration of the borrower's income, financial resources, and debt service obligations.

- Determine whether the underwriting policies provide appropriate guidance on permissible collateral, and collateral valuation guidelines and methodologies.

(c) If the bank uses credit scoring (e.g., bureau, pooled, or custom):

- Determine how the bank ensures that the model is appropriate for the target population and product offering.

- Assess the reasonableness of the process used to establish cut-offs, and determine whether management changed the cut-offs between examinations and the implications for portfolio quality and performance.

- Determine whether the policy provides for model monitoring and validation.

(d) Determine how policies and changes are communicated to staff, and assess the adequacy of the process.

(e) Evaluate the bank's process for establishing policy exception criteria and limits, and for monitoring and approving underwriting policy exceptions (e.g., underwriting standards, loan terms, score overrides, and collateral documentation).

(f) Determine the control processes in place to track and monitor policy adherence (e.g., quality assurance, MIS reports, loan review, and audit), and assess the adequacy of those processes.

(g) If the bank uses third-party vendors, including brokers and dealers, for services such as loan origination or collection, determine:

- How policies are communicated to those entities.

- The adequacy of the processes for monitoring and reporting policy adherence and performance.

(h) Determine whether the bank's policies and procedures, including those for third-party vendors, provide adequate guidance to avoid discriminatory, unfair, deceptive, predatory, and abusive lending practices[2] (e.g., lending predominantly on the value of collateral rather than the borrower's ability to service the debt, high-cost loans, and misleading disclosures).

11. Evaluate the condition and risk profile of the portfolio and individual products by reviewing historical trends and current levels of key performance indicators. Such indicators include, but are not limited to, loan balances, utilization, delinquencies, losses, recoveries, and profitability. Focus primarily on dollar balance percentages, but also consider percentages of numbers of accounts. Review performance indicators for:

- Major products, sub-products, portfolio segments, acquisition channels, and acquired portfolios.

- Third-party originators, including brokers and dealers.

- Internal performance indicator hurdles and metrics. Compare actual performance indicators with internally established objectives.

- The industry and peers, as available (e.g., American Banker's Association, Consumer Banker's Association, Risk Management Association, Visa's "Issuer Risk Key Indicators" (IRKI), Mortgage Bankers Association, Mortgage Information Corp. (MIC), and rating agency and securitization research). Compare industry indicators with bank performance.

In addition to coincident analysis,[3] consider performing vintage analysis,[4] especially if underwriting criteria, loan terms, or economic conditions have changed, and lagged analysis[5] if the portfolio exhibits significant growth. If available and well maintained, the bank's

---

[2] For additional information refer to the *Comptroller's Handbook*, "Fair Lending" booklet and OCC advisory letters 2002-3, "Guidance on Unfair or Deceptive Acts or Practices"; 2003-2, "Guidelines for National Banks to Guard Against Predatory and Abusive Lending Practices"; 2003-3, "Avoiding Predatory and Abusive Lending Practices in Brokered and Purchased Loans"; 2004-4, "Secured Credit Cards"; and 2004-10, "Credit Card Practices."

[3] Coincident analysis relies on end-of-period reported performance, e.g., delinquencies or losses in relation to total outstandings of the same date.

[4] Vintage analysis groups loans by origination time period (e.g., quarter) for analysis purposes. Performance trends are tracked for each vintage and compared to other vintages for similar time on book.

[5] Lagged analysis minimizes the effect of growth by using the current balance of the item of interest as the numerator (e.g., loans past due 30 days or more), and the outstanding balance of the portfolio being measured for some earlier date as the denominator. This earlier date is usually at least six months prior to the date of the information used in the numerator.

chronology log[6] should prove useful in determining the causes of variances.

12. Review new account application volumes, and approval and booking rates to assess portfolio growth. In addition, review new account metrics to determine the composition and quality of accounts currently being booked. Compare the quality of recent account bookings with that of accounts booked in the past. Metrics evaluated should include credit score distributions (if used), price tiers, loan-to-value/advance rate ratios, debt-to-income ratios, geographic distribution, override volume, and credit policy exceptions.

13. Evaluate the expected performance of the portfolio and the individual products through analysis of management reports, portfolio segmentation, and discussions with management. Specifically, review:

- Score distributions and trends for accounts over time, evaluating scores at application (e.g., application score and bureau score), refreshed bureau scores, and behavior scores.

- Delinquencies and losses by credit score range for each major scoring model, and whether there has been any deterioration of the good-to-bad odds.

- Trend in advance rates and the effect on performance and loss severity.

- Loan growth sources (e.g., branch, region, loan officer, and product channel such as, direct, indirect, telemarketing, direct mail, or Internet), and differences in performance by source.

- Levels and trends of policy and documentation exceptions, and the performance of accounts with exceptions versus the performance of the portfolio overall.

- Levels and trends of repossessions, foreclosures, and other real estate owned (residential).

- Volumes and trends of first and early payment defaults.

---

[6]The chronology log is a sequential record of internal and external events relevant to the credit function.

- Volumes and trends of account and balance attrition (open-end) and prepayment (closed-end).

- Management's loss forecasts.

14. Review collection department reports and activities to determine the implications for credit quality. *Note: Several of the procedures already performed also reflect collections activities (e.g., review of delinquencies and losses).*

    (a) Review roll rate[7] reports overall and by product; evaluate trends; and, if peer group performance is available, compare roll rates.

    (b) Review the criteria, volume, performance, and trends for forbearance programs (debt management plans and other fixed payment or workout programs), as well as for re-aged, extended, deferred, renewed, and rewritten accounts.

    (c) Determine the reasonableness of the bank's collection strategies and the adequacy and timeliness of the processes for making revisions.

    (d) Review the loss forecasting process and determine whether it is reasonable and reliable.

15. Assess the adequacy of MIS and reports with respect to providing management with the necessary information to monitor and manage all aspects of retail credit. Determine whether:

    - Adequate processes exist to ensure data integrity and report accuracy, and that balances and trends included in management's retail credit reports reconcile to the bank's general ledger and to the call report.

    - Various department reports are consistent, i.e., the reports show the same numbers for the same categories and time periods regardless of the unit generating the report.

    - Descriptions of key management reports are maintained and updated.

---

[7] Roll rates measure the movement of accounts and balances from one payment status to another (e.g., percentage of accounts or dollars that were current last month rolling to 30 days past due this month).

- Reports are produced to track volume and performance by product, channel, marketing initiative, and to support any test with implications for credit quality and/or performance (e.g., pricing, open-end line assignment/adjustment, advance rates). This reporting process should be fully operational before the bank offers new products or initiates tests in order to accurately monitor performance from inception.

- MIS and reports are available to clearly track volumes, performance, and trends for all types of forbearance/workout programs as well as activities such as re-aging, extensions, deferrals, renewals, and rewrites.

- Reports are clearly labeled and dated.

16. Determine whether the amount of the allowance for loan and lease losses (allowance) is adequate and whether the method of calculating the allowance is sound. Ensure that management routinely analyzes the portfolio to identify instances when the performance of a product or some other segment (e.g., workout programs) varies significantly from the performance of the portfolio overall, and that such differences are adequately incorporated into the allowance analysis. Refer to the "Allowance for Loan and Lease Losses" booklet of the *Comptroller's Handbook* for guidance, and specifically consider:

- Whether estimates and assumptions are documented and supported consistent with FFIEC guidance (OCC Bulletin 2001-37, "Policy Statement on Allowance for Loan and Lease Losses Methodologies and Documentation for Banks and Savings Institutions").

- Credit quality, including any changes to underwriting, account management, or collections that could affect future performance and credit losses.

- Historical credit performance and trends (e.g., delinquency roll rates and flow-to-loss), overall, by product, and by vintage within products.

- Level, trends, and performance of subprime and other higher-risk populations (e.g., over-limit accounts).

- Level, trends, and performance of cure or workout programs, including re-aging, extensions, deferrals, renewals, modifications, and rewrites.

- Levels and trends of bankruptcies, and the performance of bankruptcy accounts that remain on the bank's books (including both accounts that have been reaffirmed and those that have not).

- Charge-off practices, and compliance with the OCC Bulletin 2000-20, "FFIEC Uniform Retail Credit Classification and Account Management Policy."

- Whether management provides for accrued interest and fees deemed uncollectible in the allowance or in a separate reserve.

- The effects of securitization activities, if applicable.

- Economic conditions and trends.

17. Validate the preliminary risk assessment conclusions by conducting on-site transaction testing. The purpose of working these samples includes verifying adherence to bank policies; determining whether the bank maintains adequate documentation of analysis and decisions; verifying whether MIS reports accurately capture exception information; and determining whether practices exist that are inconsistent with bank policy or are not adequately depicted in existing management reports. The sample selected should be sufficient in size to reach a supportable conclusion.

Examiners conducting testing should remain alert for potential discriminatory, unfair, deceptive, abusive, and predatory lending practices (e.g., lending predominantly on the value of collateral rather than the borrower's ability to service the debt). If weaknesses or concerns are found, consult the bank's EIC or compliance examiner.

For each product being reviewed:

(a) Sample recently approved accounts to assess adherence to underwriting policy. If the bank uses credit scoring, select two samples, one sample from accounts not automatically approved (e.g., judgmental decision involved even if credit scoring is used as a tool) and one sample from accounts automatically approved.

(b) Sample recent "override" loans, i.e., exceptions to normal underwriting standards, to evaluate the adequacy and consistency of the judgmental decision process.

(c) Sample loans that were 60 days or more delinquent two months ago and are now current to determine whether the customer cured the delinquency through payments or if the account was extended or re-aged. If the latter, determine whether the action was consistent with existing bank policy, and that it complied with the FFIEC Uniform Retail Credit Classification and Account Management Policy.

(d) Sample loans that were recently extended, deferred, renewed, or rewritten for compliance with bank policy and reasonableness. Compliance with bank policy should be judged against the bank's normal underwriting guidelines with respect to loan-to-value, amortization period, debt or payment limitations, and pricing.

(e) Sample recently charged-off loans and review the borrower, payment, and collection history to determine whether the actions taken pre-charge-off were reasonable or if the practices had the effect of deferring losses.

Based on the results of transactional testing and the severity of concerns identified, determine whether the sample should be expanded. *Note: Refer to appendix A, "Transaction Testing," for additional testing suggestions.*

18.   Complete the "RCCP Checklist" in appendix C to determine the bank's level of compliance with the OCC Bulletin 2000-20, "FFIEC Uniform Retail Credit Classification and Account Management Policy."

19.   If the bank is involved in higher-risk retail lending, regardless of whether formally designated as subprime, ensure that management realistically identifies the level of risk assumed and that the allowance and capital provide sufficient support for the activity.

In addition, OCC Bulletin 1999-10, "Subprime Lending Activities" and OCC Bulletin 1999-15, "Subprime Lending: Risks and Rewards" provide guidance for the bank's policies and procedures. If the bank has a targeted subprime program with volume exceeding 25 percent of Tier I capital, review adherence to the requirements of OCC Bulletin 2001-6, "Subprime Lending."

20.   If the bank is engaged in credit card lending, complete the "Account Management and Loss Allowance Guidance Checklist" in appendix D

to determine the bank's level of compliance with OCC Bulletin 2003-01, "Account Management and Loss Allowance Guidance."

21. If the bank relies on third-party vendors for significant functions, review compliance with OCC Advisory Letter 2000-9, "Third-Party Risk," and OCC Bulletin 2001-47, "Risk Management Principles for Third-Party Relationships." If further review is warranted, refer to the "Third-Party Management" section in "Supplemental Examination Procedures."

22. If the bank offers overdraft protection plans, complete the "Overdraft Programs" section in this booklet's "Supplemental Examination Procedures."

23. Determine the effectiveness of the loan review process for retail lending. Determine the scope and frequency of the reviews and whether loan review provides a risk assessment of the quality of risk management and quantity of risk for retail lending. *Note: Refer to the loan review section in this booklet's "Supplemental Procedures — Risk Management and Control Functions" for additional detail.*

24. Review copies of the materials provided to the board of directors and relevant senior management committees to ensure that the board and senior management are adequately apprised of the condition of the retail credit portfolio and of significant decisions with implications for the quality and performance of the portfolio.

25. Fully document findings, conclusions, and recommendations in a memorandum for review and approval by the LPM examiner or the EIC. Reach a conclusion with respect to the quality of risk management, the quantity of risk, and the aggregate level and direction of risk, and include all necessary support. To accomplish these ends, complete the following procedures:

    (a) Determine whether further work needs to be completed in the retail credit area to fully assess credit risk or other risks. If so, refer to the appropriate supplemental procedures.

    (b) Provide criticized and classified asset totals to the LPM examiner or the EIC. In addition to the delinquency-based classifications outlined in the FFIEC Uniform Retail Credit Classification and Account Management Policy, consider bankruptcies, workout programs, repossessed and foreclosed assets, overdrafts, and any other segments that meet the criticized and classified definitions.

(c) Provide retail credit conclusions to the examiner responsible for assessing earnings and capital adequacy.

(d) If the bank securitizes assets, provide conclusions and supporting information about credit quality to the examiner assigned to review securitizations.

(e) If significant violations of laws, rulings, or regulations are noted, prepare write-ups for inclusion in the Report of Examination.

(f) Prepare a recommended supervisory strategy for the retail credit area.

(g) Document findings in OCC systems as appropriate.

Supplemental Examination Procedures

The supplemental procedures are organized by retail credit functional and product-specific areas. These procedures are targeted to larger, more complex operations, as well as to smaller banks whose condition requires more comprehensive review.

Note: Examiners should select the appropriate procedures necessary to assess the condition and risk of the bank's retail lending products and operations.

Management Planning

Objective: Assess the effectiveness of the overall planning process and the bank's capacity, including management expertise and staffing, with respect to retail credit products offered and planned.

1.   Discuss the bank's planning process with management and determine whether the process is formal or informal. The applicability of the following steps will depend upon the size and complexity of the bank and the process in place.

2.   Determine whether the retail credit component of the strategic plan is realistic and prudent given the current competitive, economic, and legal environments, and the bank's capacity and level of expertise.

   (a) Assess the strategy and any supporting documents.

   (b) Determine whether the retail credit objectives are consistent with the bank's strategic plan.

   (c) Determine whether marketing plans and budgets for retail lending are consistent with the retail credit objectives and the bank's strategic plan.

   (d) Review the competitive analysis (bank-prepared) and available industry information.

   (e) Review the analysis of economic, legal, and other external factors.

   (f) Review the assumptions used to develop the plan and assess the reasonableness of the assumptions.

(g) Review the organizational structure and management expertise in key positions; determine whether they are adequate to execute the plan (incorporating conclusions regarding capacity).

3.   Determine whether the strategy establishes realistic risk tolerances.

    (a) Determine whether the plan incorporates risk parameters for growth, credit quality, concentrations, income, and capital.

    (b) Determine how the limits were established (e.g., assumptions used).

    (c) Assess the limits for reasonableness.

    (d) Discuss the key risks and obstacles (strengths, weaknesses, opportunities, and challenges) to achieving the plan with management.

4.   Assess the adequacy of the bank's process for tracking performance against the plan.

    (a) Determine the process to track actual performance against the plan.

    (b) Assess the adequacy of the process, including:

        – The timeliness, accuracy, and detail of reports.

        – Frequency of reports.

        – Report distribution, ensuring that results are provided to senior management and the board.

    (c) Assess the bank's process for revising the plan and supporting operating or product plans to reflect current information and trends.

5.   Determine whether management adequately considers the economic cycle in the planning process.

    (a) If the bank does not incorporate such information, determine whether planning is appropriate given the bank's circumstances (e.g., size and complexity of operation, market).

    (b) Determine who develops the scenarios (e.g., finance, marketing, or risk management), and obtain copies of the best, worst, and most likely scenarios.

    (c) Review the assumptions used, the reasonableness of the assumptions, and the frequency of analyses.

(d) Determine whether the bank uses stress testing. If the bank does not have such a process, discuss with management how the portfolio would withstand an economic downturn. For example, how does the bank ensure that underwriting standards are maintained at levels sufficient to withstand economic cycles?

(e) Determine how management uses this information in the planning process.

(f) If warranted, recommend that the bank adopt stress testing.

6. Determine whether the bank has sufficient management expertise and whether management is held accountable for executing the plan.

(a) Using the organization chart, discuss the backgrounds and responsibilities of key managers with senior management. Confirm understanding of those roles with the key managers.

(b) Obtain the criteria for key management compensation programs and position evaluations or performance elements. Determine whether they include appropriate qualitative (risk) considerations in addition to quantitative (growth or marketing) goals, and whether the goals are consistent with the bank's plan. In addition, review key managers' performance-based compensation for the most recent evaluation period to ensure that managers are, in fact, held accountable for meeting agreed-upon objectives.

(c) Incorporate the results from the other examination objectives in reaching conclusions regarding management.

7. Determine whether the operational capacity, infrastructure, and MIS are sufficient to support and execute the bank's strategic plan.

(a) Determine whether key operations and systems managers are adequately involved in the planning process.

(b) Discuss capacity planning with management (e.g., facilities, systems, staffing, and training).

(c) If available, obtain and review the most recent capacity studies for staffing (including underwriting, collections, and control functions), facilities, systems, and technology. Assess adequacy, and identify the implications for plan execution. Assess management's response to study findings, and the potential impact on current plans.

(d) Review the retail organizational structure and note any significant changes in senior management or staffing levels, including turnover trends for significant functional areas.

(e) Review the compensation plans in place for the various functional areas (e.g., sales/originations, collections), and assess the reasonableness of those plans.

(f) Incorporate the results from the other examiners assigned to the review; determine whether any capacity, infrastructure, or MIS issues/problems have been revealed.

8. Ensure that management has a process for establishing specific performance goals for items such as loan growth, policy overrides, credit performance, and profitability for the retail portfolio as a whole and segmented by product. Determine whether management effectively tracks actual performance against these goals.

9. Determine whether management has appropriately considered loan loss allowance and capital needs and support in the plan.

10. Develop conclusions with respect to the effectiveness of the overall planning process and the bank's capacity, including management expertise and staffing, with respect to retail credit products offered and planned.

Marketing and Product Development

Objective: Determine whether marketing activities are consistent with the bank's business plans, strategic plans, and risk tolerance objectives, and that appropriate controls and systems are in place before the bank rolls out new products or new-product marketing initiatives.

1. Assess the structure and expertise of marketing, focusing on management, key personnel, and staffing adequacy.

2. Review the bank's marketing plan and assess it for reasonableness given the bank's strategic plan and objectives, level of expertise, capacity (operational and financial resources), market area, and competition.

(a) Determine whether the bank bases its plan on internally or externally prepared market, economic, or profitability studies. If so, obtain and review copies of those studies.

(b) Review the process for developing and implementing marketing plans, with particular attention to whether the appropriate functional areas (e.g., risk management, finance, operations, information technology, legal, and compliance) are involved throughout the process.

(c) Assess the appropriateness of the data and assumptions used to develop marketing plans, in part through the review of MIS reports that track actual performance against marketing plans.

(d) Discuss with management the controls in place to monitor marketing plans and activities.

Note: Prior to the implementation of any marketing initiative, including the rollout of a new product or change to an existing product, management should review all marketing materials, consumer disclosures, and product features and terms to identify and address potential discriminatory, unfair, deceptive, abusive, and predatory lending practices.[8]

(e) Discuss with management any significant changes made or planned to the bank's account acquisition, account management, and cross-selling strategies, including changes in channels and the use of third-party vendors.

3. Assess new product development. Specifically:

(a) Discuss with management the new product development process.

(b) Determine whether there are written guidelines for what constitutes a new product.

(c) Review new product proposals and plans approved since the last examination.

(d) Determine whether the appropriate functional areas (e.g., risk management, finance, operations, information technology, legal,

---

[8] For additional information refer to the *Comptroller's Handbook,* "Fair Lending" booklet *and* OCC advisory letters 2002-3, "Guidance on Unfair or Deceptive Acts or Practices"; 2003-2, "Guidelines for National Banks to Guard Against Predatory and Abusive Lending Practices"; 2003-3, "Avoiding Predatory and Abusive Lending Practices in Brokered and Purchased Loans"; 2004-4, "Secured Credit Cards"; and 2004-10, "Credit Card Practices."

and compliance) are involved throughout the development process to ensure that associated risks are properly identified and controlled. In addition, determine whether the constituents remain involved during implementation.

(e) Evaluate systems planning to determine whether MIS and reporting needs are adequately researched and developed before new products are rolled out. Specifically, determine whether the systems and reports are adequate to supervise and administer new products.

(f) Evaluate the adequacy of the review and approval processes for new products.

(g) Determine whether management, including appropriate legal and compliance personnel, reviews marketing materials during the product development and implementation to avoid deceptive or misleading advertising, terms, and disclosures.

(h) Determine whether the planning process adequately identifies and addresses the risks, operational needs, and systems support associated with different solicitation methods and channels, including direct applications, preapproved offers, indirect (broker/dealer), loan-by-phone, and the Internet.

4.   Evaluate the adequacy of the bank's test process for new products, marketing campaigns, and other significant initiatives. Review the process to ensure that testing:

- Is a required step for any new products or significant marketing and account management initiatives.

- Is properly approved. Senior management should approve the testing plan, and it should determine that the proposed test is consistent with the bank's strategic plan and meets strategic objectives.

- Requires clear descriptions of test objectives and methods (e.g., assumptions, test size and selection criteria, and duration), as well as key performance measurements and targets.

- Includes a strong test and control discipline. The test must include a clean holdout group and test groups that are not subject to any significant account management or cross-selling initiatives for the duration of the test. *Note: Strict test group design enables management to draw more accurate performance conclusions.*

- Is accorded an adequate period of time, sufficient to determine probable performance and to work through any operational or other issues. When the test involves a significant departure from existing bank products or practices, test duration should probably be longer.

  Note: Tests should run at least six months, and should usually run nine months or twelve months. The time frame may vary depending on the product or practice being tested.

- Is supported by appropriate MIS and reporting prior to implementation.

- Requires a thorough and well-supported postmortem analysis in which results are presented to and approved by senior management and the board before full rollout.

5. Determine whether management assesses how underwriting standards for the new products may affect credit risk and the bank's risk profile.

6. Evaluate cross-selling strategies, including the criteria used to select accounts.

7. If the bank maintains a data warehouse, determine how it is used for marketing purposes and if it is capable of aggregating customer loan relationships.

8. Determine the adequacy and effectiveness of the bank's controls with respect to information sharing, for both affiliates and unrelated third parties.

9. Prepare profiles for each of the products offered. Address:

- Product description, including any unique characteristics and a general overview of terms (including pricing), target market (credit quality and geographic), and distribution channels.

- Changes in the product characteristics since the last examination.

- Volume and trends summary, discussing growth to date and planned.

10. Select at least one new product introduced since the prior supervisory activity to assess the bank's planning process. Specifically, review:

- The planning documents and the final approved proposal.

- Tests and analysis conducted, including performance compared to expectations.

- MIS tracking reports.

- Available risk management, quality assurance, and audit reviews.

- Any subsequent product modifications and the basis/documented support for those changes.

- Management review and approval documentation.

- Information presented to the Board of Directors.

11. Develop conclusions about whether marketing activities are consistent with the bank's business plans, strategic plans, and risk tolerance objectives, and whether appropriate controls and systems are in place before new products or marketing initiatives are rolled out.

Underwriting

Objective: Assess the quality of the bank's new loans and any changes from past underwriting; determine the adequacy of and adherence to retail credit lending policies and procedures; and gain a thorough understanding of the processes employed in account origination.

1. Ascertain and evaluate the types of lending and leasing the bank engages in, and evaluate the reasonableness of the following:

- Loan products offered and planned.

- Underwriting standards and terms.

- Degree of innovation (e.g., new terms, products, and markets).

- Markets served and economic conditions.

- Competitive environment.

- Volume and proportion of loan portfolio (managed and on book), by product.

- Level of participation in high-risk or subprime lending.

- Types of marketing and account acquisition channels.

- Historical and planned growth.

- Securitization activities.

Note: When evaluating lending activities, examiners should remain alert for practices and product terms that could indicate discriminatory, unfair, deceptive, abusive, or predatory issues.

2. Review new account metrics to determine the composition and quality of accounts currently being booked and the adequacy of MIS to track new loan volume. Compare the quality of recent bookings to the quality of accounts booked in the past. Metrics evaluated, by product, should include:

- Application volume, and approval and booking rates.

- Distribution of credit scores, if used, by applications, approved, and booked.

- Price tiers and fees.

- Loan-to-value/advance rate ratios.

- Average loan amount.

- Initial utilization or draw rate (open-end credit).

- Debt-to-income and/or payment-to-income ratios.

- Geographic distribution.

- Override volume.

- Credit policy exceptions.

3. Obtain an overview of the origination process and the steps involved, including application receipt and processing, underwriting, and collateral perfection and documentation. When describing the process in the work papers, document the following:

(a) Which aspects of the underwriting process are automated versus manual.

(b) Use of credit scoring models (e.g., types of models, history of model use, monitoring, and validation).

(c) Differences in the underwriting processes arising from the application channel (i.e., direct mail, telemarketing, Internet, and broker/dealer), and the differences for unsolicited versus pre-qualified or pre-approved applications.

(d) How security interests are perfected, who is responsible, and how filings are tracked.[i]

(e) Whether insurance coverage is verified and whether it is monitored thereafter.

4.   Determine how management evaluates underwriter performance, including monitoring new loan MIS and subsequent performance MIS by underwriter, and transaction testing completed for each underwriter by the manager, quality assurance, and loan review.

5.   If the bank uses credit scoring in the underwriting process, assess the mix of automated and judgmentally approved loans. Also, refer to the credit scoring steps in the "Risk Management and Control Functions" section of the "Supplemental Examination Procedures."

6.   For banks that lend in multiple geographic areas/states, confirm that management performs periodic bureau preference analyses to determine optimal credit bureaus for different states or localities.

7.   Obtain a copy of the bank's retail credit lending policies and procedures. Assess the adequacy and soundness of the policies and procedures, focusing on the main criteria used in the decision-making process and, if applicable, the verification processes used to confirm application and/or transaction information. Evaluate:

- Permissible types of loans.

- Lending authority and limits, and the exception approval process.

- Limits on concentrations of credit (e.g., product, geographic, broker, dealer, and score band).

- Credit underwriting criteria, including measurements of the borrower's capacity to repay the loan (e.g., debt-to-income and payment-to-income ratios) and treatment of derogatory credit bureau items.

- Credit scorecard cut-offs and tolerances for overrides.

- Borrower credit grade definitions (e.g., A, B, and C).
- Repayment terms (e.g., duration, amortization schedule, and pricing).
- Maximum amount financed and loan-to-value (LTV) ratios, including allowable options and verification of options and add-ons, as applicable.
- Permissible collateral (furniture, automobiles, service contracts) and lien perfection requirements.
- Collateral valuation guidelines and methodologies.
- Exception and override processes, criteria, and tracking.

8. Determine whether the policies and procedures provide adequate guidance to avoid discriminatory, unfair, deceptive, abusive, and predatory lending practices. Policies and procedures should address, if applicable, the circumstances in which the bank may make loans involving features or actions that have been associated with discriminatory, unfair, deceptive, abusive, and predatory lending practices, including:

- Lending predominantly on the liquidation value of collateral rather than the borrower's ability to service the debt.
- Refinancing loans frequently.
- Refinancing special subsidized mortgages that contain terms favorable to the borrower.
- Requiring single-premium credit life insurance or similar products.
- Using negative amortization.
- Requiring balloon payments in short-term transactions.
- Charging prepayment penalties in the later years of a loan.
- Charging high financing points, fees, and penalties.
- Increasing interest rates upon default.
- Inserting mandatory arbitration clauses.

- Making high-cost loans (e.g., loans subject to the Home Ownership and Equity Protection Act[9]).

Additionally, policies and procedures should provide adequate guidance to ensure that loans offered to borrowers are consistent with their needs, objectives, and financial condition.

If weaknesses or concerns are found, consult the bank's EIC or compliance examiner.

Note: For additional information refer to the Comptroller's Handbook, "Fair Lending" booklet and OCC Advisory Letters, 2002-3, "Guidance on Unfair or Deceptive Acts or Practices"; 2003-2, "Guidelines for National Banks to Guard Against Predatory and Abusive Lending Practices"; 2003-3, "Avoiding Predatory and Abusive Lending Practices in Brokered and Purchased Loans"; 2004-4, "Secured Credit Cards"; and 2004-10, "Credit Card Practices."

9.   Assess the adequacy of the process for changing underwriting standards. Review all changes in standards since the last examination, and determine their effect on the quality of the loan portfolio.

   (a) Review analyses and documentation supporting recent changes to underwriting criteria and score cut-offs.

   (b) Discuss reasons for changes (if not readily apparent) with bank management and determine whether there has been a shift in the credit risk appetite.

   (c) Determine whether all affected functional areas provide input to underwriting changes.

   (d) Verify that management maintains a chronology of significant changes to underwriting standards.

10.   Determine the adequacy of the bank's verification procedures and verify that, at a minimum, residence, employment, income, and collateral values are routinely confirmed for subprime borrowers.

---

[9] The Home Ownership and Equity Protection Act (HOEPA) imposes specific disclosure requirements and substantive restrictions on closed-end loans secured by a consumer's principal dwelling, other than a reverse mortgage or a loan to finance the acquisition or initial construction of the home, that are high-cost because they exceed specified federal statutory and regulatory interest rate and fee thresholds. See 15 USC 1639 and 12 CFR 226.32.

11.	Evaluate credit policy exception and scorecard override limits and tracking/reporting. Determine whether:

(a) Volumes conform to policy limits, and that those limits are reasonable.

(b) Management tracks the volumes and trends of policy exceptions (by type) and overrides separately and by reason code.

(c) Management tracks the performance (i.e., delinquencies and losses) of these accounts over time, by type, and compares the performance to that of the overall portfolio.

(d) As warranted, management responds appropriately to the levels of overrides and exceptions, adjusting underwriting policies and exception limits or providing additional underwriter training accordingly.

(e) Management appropriately identifies the effects of the levels of exceptions and overrides and the performance of affected accounts on the quantity and direction of credit risk.

12.	Determine whether the volume of collateral exceptions is reasonable and is tracked appropriately and whether the impact is assessed.

13.	Determine how management tracks lapsed insurance coverage, and how management addresses coverage lapses (e.g., contacting borrowers to reinstate insurance, requiring forced-place insurance, or maintaining third-party insurance coverage on the portfolio). If forced-place insurance is used, determine whether management tracks unpaid premiums.

14.	Select and work appropriate samples to determine credit quality; to verify adherence to bank underwriting policies, including verification procedures; to assess the adequacy of analysis and decision documentation; to determine that MIS reports accurately capture exception information; and to determine whether practices exist that are inconsistent with bank policy or that are not adequately depicted in existing management reports. For each significant product type:

(a) Sample recently approved accounts to assess adherence to underwriting policy. If the bank uses credit scoring, select two samples, one sample from accounts not automatically approved (e.g., judgmental decision involved even if credit scoring is used as a tool) and one sample from accounts automatically approved. Ensure that your sample includes loans originated from each significant marketing channel and, if warranted, consider expanding the sample to more thoroughly test specific channels.

(b) Sample recently approved accounts that represent exceptions to underwriting policy to determine whether credit decisions are consistent and whether the analysis and other support for them is adequate.

(c) If the bank uses brokers, dealers, or other third-party originators (TPOs), sample recently approved loans from each significant TPO, with emphasis on loans made with exceptions, if any. Assess adherence to bank policy, consistency of decision making, and adequacy of supporting documentation.

Use the bank's credit files, account origination systems, and MIS reports to create a worksheet to summarize information for the sample. The worksheet should be tailored to fit the product and the bank's underwriting criteria, but will generally include the following information:

- Account data — name, account number, origination date, employment information, time at residence.

- Underwriting terms — credit score (bureau, pooled, and/or custom), debt-to-income, loan-to-value, pricing, loan term, payment amount.

- Collateral information — invoice price and options (automobiles), appraised value and lien information (real estate), insurance verification.

- Underwriting policy exceptions and score overrides (indicate whether bank or examiner identified).

If prepared properly, the worksheet will facilitate examiner analysis and provide a sound foundation for reaching conclusions about the adequacy of the bank's policy and adherence thereto.

15. Based on the results of the testing and the severity of the concerns identified, determine whether the samples should be expanded. Refer to appendix A, "Transaction Testing," for additional sample suggestions.

16.   Develop conclusions with respect to the quality of the bank's new loans, any changes from past underwriting, the adequacy of and adherence to retail credit lending policies and procedures, the processes employed in account origination, MIS for monitoring new loan volume, and implications for the risk profile of the loan portfolio. Clearly document all findings.

Third-Party Originations (Includes Brokers and Dealers)

Note: Also see "Third-Party Management" in the "Supplemental Examination Procedures" for information on contracts, due diligence, and performance monitoring.

17.   Determine whether the bank has underwriting guidelines and governing contracts for purchasing loans originated by third parties and assess the reasonableness of those guidelines. Verify that the bank has the ability to reject loans that do not meet its criteria.

18.   Determine the adequacy of processes in place, including quality control, to ensure that purchased loans are consistent with the bank's underwriting criteria. Specifically, determine:

- How policies are communicated to third parties.

- The adequacy of the policy adherence, performance monitoring processes, and reporting.

19.   Assess the adequacy of the bank's process for establishing relationships with brokers, dealers, and other origination sources. *Note: Be alert to any insider and affiliate relationships, conflicts of interest, concentrations, and the originators' ability to perform on recourse commitments.*

(a) Review the bank's due diligence process and qualification requirements.

(b) Sample new and significant existing relationships, and review the file documentation and agreements to determine adherence to due diligence and qualification requirements.

20.   Evaluate the broker and dealer monitoring process. Determine whether:

(a) MIS and reports provide sufficient information to track and evaluate the performance of individual brokers and dealers, including:

- The volume of applications, approvals, and bookings.

- Booking quality (e.g., credit scores or grades).

- Exceptions and overrides.

- Credit performance (e.g., delinquencies, losses, first or early payment defaults, and repossessions).

- Profitability.

(b) Management performs annual or periodic reviews of brokers and dealers.

(c) Management maintains a broker and dealer watch list and terminates relationships that are not meeting underwriting guidelines and quality standards.

21. Evaluate dealer reserve arrangements and the procedures for managing those reserves. Review the adequacy of the bank's procedures for advancing dealer differentials and for recovering advances on early payoffs and defaults.

Vehicle Loans and Leases

22. Review management's process for identifying and monitoring portfolio concentrations (e.g., make, model, type, maturity, LTVs greater than 100 percent, and roll-in of prior vehicle's loan balance). Discuss with management the risks of any significant concentrations, such as a high percentage of sports utility vehicles or a significant percentage of the portfolio maturing within a given time frame.

23. Determine whether the bank carries material volumes of lease-like loans[10] and incorporate this information into the leasing and residual risk[11] analysis.

---

[10] Lease-like loans are loans with a put option that allows the customer to return the vehicle to the bank at maturity. Because of the put option, the bank is exposed to residual risk. Lease-like-loans are most common in states where higher taxes are imposed on leased vehicles, or in states with onerous liability statutes.

[11] Residual risk is the bank's exposure to the vehicle's fair value falling below management's residual value estimate.

24. If the bank is engaged in leasing and offers lease-to-loan or lease-to-lease products at the end of the lease term, evaluate the reasonableness of the underwriting criteria used. Be particularly sensitive to whether the activity allows for refinancing or renewing at amounts more than the value of the vehicle.

25. Review lease discounting (booking operations). Determine whether management has developed:

    - Adequate processes for verifying key elements of the transaction (e.g., cap costs, residual values, and fees).

    - MIS reports to track and evaluate the effectiveness of the discounting process.

    - Proper staffing levels in high-growth situations.

26. Assess the adequacy of the bank's policies, procedures, and practices with respect to lease residuals.

    (a) Determine whether lease residual values are established using guidebook values (e.g., ALG or Kelly) or some other method, and assess the reasonableness of the process and the values assigned.

    (b) Determine whether the bank enhances or adjusts guidebook values. If so, review the method and supporting documentation, and assess the underlying rationale. Examples of enhancements include:

        - Adding dealer-installed optional equipment that is not consistent with guidebook add-ons.

        - Using a value that exceeds the maximum recommended MSRP.

        - Originating an odd-term lease (such as 39 months), but basing the residual value on a 36-month maturity.

        - Allowing free or bonus mileage.

    (c) Review compliance with FAS 13, Accounting for Leases, by determining whether:

        - Management reviews residual values at least annually.

        - Management uses appropriate assumptions in its reviews.

        - Any other than temporary impairment identified during the management reviews is expensed.

- Any write-downs are not subsequently revised upward.

(d) Review any residual value insurance programs, including:

- Management's process for selecting coverage.

- The type of insurance in place (e.g., catastrophic, full, full with deductible, and deductible), and any limitations or exclusions.

- Basis for determining premiums.

- Historical trends of insurance claims versus premiums paid by book of business.

- Basis for approving or denying insurance claims.

If time permits, test submitted claims that have been denied, partially paid, and paid in full.

27. Review the appropriateness of bank management procedures for determining if a lease transaction should be accounted for as a direct finance lease or an operating lease.

Real Estate Secured Loans

28. For loans secured by residential real estate, assess the adequacy of the bank's appraisal and collateral valuation processes as follows:

(a) Review the bank's residential real estate lending appraisal and evaluation policies and procedures to assess the appropriateness of the collateral valuation program.

(b) Ascertain the types of valuation methods used to determine collateral values.

(c) Determine why the bank uses one method versus another, and assess the reasonableness and adequacy of the method(s) employed and the supporting rationale. *Note: Banks typically consider costs, timeliness, and accuracy.*

(d) Determine how management monitors the quality and certifications of appraisers, how appraisers are added to or deleted from the approved appraiser list, and whether the bank maintains an appraiser "watch list" to monitor marginal appraisers. Also determine how management selects and monitors the performance of individuals who perform evaluations.

(e) If the bank uses tools such as automated valuation models (AVMs) or tax assessment values to meet evaluation requirements, determine the extent of usage (i.e., for portfolio management or to underwrite individual transactions). Also ascertain how management evaluates and ensures the accuracy and validity of these valuation tools on an ongoing basis.

(f) Ascertain compliance with 12 CFR 34, ensuring that:

- Appraisals and valuations meet regulatory requirements and content standards discussed in the "Interagency Appraisal and Evaluation Guidelines," issued October 27, 1994. Refer to appendix E of the *Comptroller's Handbook*, "Commercial Real Estate and Construction Lending" booklet.

- The bank maintains an effective compliance review function.

- Independence for ordering and reviewing the appraisals and valuations is maintained.

- Loans and lines made in excess of supervisory loan-to-value limits are tracked in aggregate, do not exceed 100 percent of capital when combined with other loans in excess of supervisory limits, and are reported to the board of directors quarterly.

(g) Determine the adequacy of the appraisal quality control process, including loan coverage and re-appraisals (triggering criteria and appraisers used) or re-evaluations.

(h) If mortgage brokers, correspondents, or other third parties are used to source transactions, ascertain that controls are in place to monitor their compliance with the bank's underwriting and standards for valuation independence.

Account Management

Objective: Assess the effectiveness of activities and strategies used to enhance performance and increase profitability of existing, nondelinquent accounts or portfolios, and determine the implications for the quality of the portfolio and the quantity and direction of risk.

Note: Account management activities are used extensively in open-end lending for products such as credit cards, home equity lines, and other unsecured lines of credit. However, banks should actively monitor and manage existing closed-end accounts as well. Therefore, the following procedures, while more applicable to open-end products, include aspects relevant for closed-end products.

1. Determine whether bank systems are capable of aggregating the entire loan relationship by customer (multiple loan accounts by product and in total) for the purpose of customer-level account management. If so, determine the extent to which the bank uses that capability.

2. Determine whether the bank uses credit scoring for nondelinquent account management. If so, identify the type of scoring used (e.g., refreshed bureau, behavior, and bankruptcy scores), the frequency of obtaining updated scores, and how the scores are used in the account management process.

3. If the bank does not use or augments scoring, determine how management reviews the bank's account base for changes in credit quality (e.g., bureau warning screens or delinquent property tax notifications) or to identify marketing opportunities. Determine whether the process is reasonable, including any actions taken based on the reviews.

4. Review and assess the adequacy of written policies and procedures, including disclosure requirements, governing account management activities. Account management activities may include:

    - Bureau-based,[12] performance-based,[13] and other re-pricing initiatives.

    - Line increase and decrease programs.

    - Line suspension, convert to amortization, and closure programs.

---

[12] Bureau-based re-pricing refers to finance charge changes made to existing accounts based on changes in borrower creditworthiness identified through shifts in credit bureau scores or other credit bureau information (tied to customer's performance with all creditors). While the technique can be used to adjust the finance charge up or down, it is most often used to increase pricing.

[13] Performance-based re-pricing refers to finance charge changes made in response to borrower performance on the account with the creditor. The strategy typically relies on internal behavior scores and delinquency patterns, but may also incorporate a number of factors including line utilization and bureau score. Like bureau-based analysis, performance-based analysis can be used to increase or decrease finance charges, but is frequently associated with default price increases. When employed for delinquent accounts, there is often a provision to return to a lower finance charge following a specified period of sustained on-time payments.

- Graduation programs.[14]

- Balance transfer and convenience check offers.

- Payment holiday programs.

- Pay ahead programs.[15]

- Customer service re-ages, extensions, and deferrals.

- Retention programs. *Note: Retention programs are critical to relationship management and attrition. Be alert to whether the programs are proactive or reactive, and how management measures performance.*

5. Determine the adequacy of the bank's administration of account management programs. Specifically:

    (a) Review the adequacy of the program or strategy approval process and assess whether all interested units are appropriately represented (e.g., risk management, marketing, customer service, compliance, information technology, and finance).

    (b) Assess whether the analyses performed to support new and existing strategies are adequate and appropriately consider all possible effects of the proposed actions (e.g., the effects on credit performance, attrition and adverse retention, earnings, and compliance and reputation risks). In addition, determine whether analyses properly consider the impact of overlapping or repeat account management strategies.

    (c) Determine whether the bank performs adequate testing of strategies that have the potential for significant impact on credit performance and earnings prior to full implementation. Testing is particularly important for re-pricing and line management initiatives, and should

---

[14] In open-end credit, graduation programs reward sustained successful performance of high-risk borrowers by moving them from a subprime type of account (typically higher priced, lower credit limit, and often secured) to a more mainstream product.

[15] Pay ahead refers to the application of excess payment amounts to the next consecutive payment(s). As a result, the customer will not be required to make payments until the amount of the overage has been extinguished. For example, if a customer's automobile payment is $200 per month, but the customer remits $600, the next payment will not be due until the third subsequent month. This practice is generally discouraged in other than prearranged situations (vacations, etc.); excess payments should be applied to the principal balance thus reducing the number of total payments rather than interrupting the regular payment stream.

be conducted for a minimum of six months, but preferably for twelve months.

(d) Ensure that the bank has developed and implemented appropriate MIS reports prior to initiating testing and strategies, and that management regularly monitors and analyzes actual versus expected results.

(e) Assess the adequacy and timeliness of management's response to poorly performing strategies, as well as the actions taken when strategies perform significantly better than expected.

6. Assess the reasonableness of the bank's account management strategies, evaluating the scope and frequency of each strategy employed, the inclusion and exclusion criteria, the various strategy components and outcomes, and adherence to the approved proposals and written policies and procedures. *Note: Keep in mind that payment holiday programs should only be offered to the most creditworthy customers, and that pay-ahead programs are discouraged.*

7. Review the policies that govern imposing and waiving late, over-limit, extension, annual, and other fees. Determine whether the policies are reasonable, and that the effect on performance is adequately monitored, analyzed, and acted upon.

8. Based on the significance of the bank's use of account management activities, determine whether account sampling is warranted. If so, refer to the sampling procedures below and in appendix A, "Transaction Testing."

9. Develop conclusions with respect to the effectiveness of activities and strategies used to enhance performance and profitability of existing, nondelinquent accounts or portfolios, and any implications for the quality of the portfolio and the quantity and direction of risk. Clearly document all findings.

Open-End Credit (Credit Cards and Home Equity Lines of Credit)

10. Evaluate the adequacy of the bank's transaction authorization process, assessing transaction limits (e.g., dollar amount, frequency, and cash

versus purchase allocations), and criteria used to "block" accounts (prohibit additional transactions). In addition:

(a) Ascertain the types of transactions (e.g., small dollar transactions, recurring transactions, delayed postings, such as rental cars) that are likely to circumvent the bank's authorization process and determine how the bank manages that risk.

(b) Determine how the bank handles payments returned for insufficient funds, and the adequacy of the bank's policies for large payment holds.

(c) For home equity lines of credit, determine how the bank handles the line when a borrower's creditworthiness deteriorates or the property value declines.

11. Determine whether the bank allows borrowers to exceed their credit limits. If so:

(a) Determine the amount and reasonableness of the over-limit authorization buffers, if any.

(b) Assess the bank's over-limit strategies, focusing on how the eligibility criteria are developed, whether the strategies are appropriately tested, the adequacy of the initial and ongoing analyses supporting the strategies, and the management approval process for the program.

(c) Assess the adequacy of over-limit MIS reporting and assess whether it provides accurate data reflecting over-limit volume, trends, and the subsequent performance of over-limit accounts.

(d) Review the requirements of the account terms and conditions for curing over-limits and determine whether the bank enforces these requirements. Assess the adequacy of the bank's process.

For credit card accounts, assess the bank's compliance with the over-limit requirements of OCC Bulletin 2003-1, "Account Management and Loss Allowance Guidance." Refer to appendix D, "Account Management and Loss Allowance Guidance Checklist."

12. Review internal reports on over-limit activity. If the volume is significant or if negative trends are evident, discuss with management.

13. Conduct transaction testing to verify the initial conclusions on the prudence of the bank's account management strategies. Determine whether the accounts reviewed are performing consistent with program assumptions and expectations and whether the action resulted in a change in credit risk. In addition, determine whether accounts conform to initiative criteria, MIS reports accurately capture tracking information, and management has adequately identified and controlled the impact of repeat and competing strategies:

(a) Sample accounts from at least one of the significant bureau and performance-based re-pricing initiatives since the last examination. In addition to the items mentioned above, determine whether the accounts received other price increases in the last 12 to 18 months and whether the accounts also received line increases or other favorable account treatment during that time. Identify current or probable performance issues and, if possible, causes.

   Note: When selecting the initiative to sample, consider the size of the population affected, the amount of the change, or the initiative with the greatest performance variance from program projections. Place emphasis on the older initiatives with characteristics similar to current initiatives in order to gain the longest subsequent performance period.

(b) Sample accounts from at least one of the significant automated line increase and decrease initiatives since the prior supervisory activity. Consider the factors listed in (a) in selecting the sample initiatives and in working the sample. For real estate secured lines, determine the validity of the bank's valuation method and compliance with 12 CFR 34.

(c) Sample accounts that exceed approved credit limits by a certain threshold (e.g., accounts 10 percent or more over the limit) as of the last statement or billing date. Determine why the accounts are over the limit (e.g., authorization, insufficient funds, or other issues); when the bank imposes or suspends over-limit fees; how the minimum payment is calculated; and whether practices are consistent with the disclosures in the account's terms and conditions. In addition, determine whether negative amortization exists and, if so, the extent thereof.

(d) Sample accounts that received manual line increases or decreases, price increases, or other significant treatment, and assess whether the policies were consistently applied and whether the analyses and decisions were well-documented.

Clearly document the sample review and findings in the work papers.

Closed-End Credit (Vehicle and Real Estate Loans)

14. Determine how the bank handles payments returned for insufficient funds or other reasons. Verify that accounts are returned to the appropriate delinquency status if the payment instrument does not clear.

15. Evaluate the adequacy of the bank's process for handling voluntary collateral turn-ins for current loans. Specifically, determine the bank's process for valuing the collateral, taking associated charge-offs, and dealing with deficiency balances.

16. Determine whether the bank will renew, modify, or rewrite existing loans to nondelinquent customers. If so, evaluate the adequacy of the process, including the policies and procedures employed and the volume, trends, and subsequent performance of those loans.

17. Assess the adequacy of the bank's process for monitoring ongoing insurance coverage and the loss payee status on collateral.

Collections

Objective: Evaluate the effectiveness of the collection function, including the collection strategies and programs employed, to better assess the quality of the portfolio and the quantity and direction of credit risk.

General

1. Assess the structure, management, and staffing of the collections department. If not previously performed:

   (a) Review the organization chart for the department and evaluate the quality and depth of the staff based on the size and complexity of the operation.

   (b) Discuss with senior management staffing plans for each major collection activity (e.g., early stage, late stage, fraud, and agency management - both third-party collection and credit counseling agencies), including how plans fit with department and bank objectives (e.g., growth and credit performance projections).

(c) Review the experience levels of senior managers and supervisors.

(d) Assess the adequacy of the bank's training program for collectors through discussions with management.

(e) Assess the appropriateness and administration of the bank's incentive pay program for collectors. Pay particular attention to possible negative ramifications of the plan, such as the potential to encourage protracted repayment plans, aggressive curing of accounts, or individual rather than team efforts. Determine whether the plan limits the total incentive pay a collector can receive.

(f) Determine whether the board or senior management reviewed and approved the incentive pay program prior to implementation.

2. Assess the adequacy of the bank's written collection policies and procedures. Determine whether they cover all significant collection activities and comply with OCC Bulletin 2000-20, "FFIEC Uniform Retail Credit Classification and Account Management Policy" and OCC Bulletin 2003-01, "Account Management and Loss Allowance Guidance." Refer to the checklists in appendixes C and D.

(a) Verify that the bank's policies prohibit the rebooking of accounts that are charged off for anything other than bank error.

(b) Determine whether the bank is considered a debt collector as defined by the Fair Debt Collection Practices Act. If so, ensure appropriate review at the next compliance examination.

(c) Identify where management has implemented automated decisions (i.e., charge-off, re-aging, extensions) to comply with the above policy guidelines.

3. Evaluate the adequacy of the bank's classification, nonaccrual, and charge-off practices and whether the practices comply with the bank's written policies and procedures. Specifically:

(a) Discuss practices with both management and line personnel. Identify any inconsistencies with policies and procedures versus practices. Ensure examiners assisting with the collection review and conducting testing are aware of these inconsistencies.

(b) Identify where management has implemented automated processes versus manual processes to comply with policies. Review the system settings to verify that the parameters correspond to those described in the bank's policies and allow compliance with FFIEC policies. If not, discuss the differences with management and request appropriate corrective action.

(c) Request management's summary of classified retail and residential real estate loans. Determine if the classification practices comply with OCC Bulletin 2000-20, "FFIEC Uniform Retail Credit Classification and Account Management Policy." Generally, all retail loans and certain residential real estate loans should be classified substandard at 90 days past due.

(d) Request management's summary of nonaccrual retail and residential real estate loans. If the bank does not place retail and residential real estate loans on nonaccrual, determine that the bank employs appropriate methods to ensure income is accurately measured (e.g., loss allowances for uncollectible fees and finance charges).

(e) Determine how accounts scheduled for charge-off are loaded into a charge-off queue or other system for loss. Specifically, determine whether losses are automatically or manually processed, what circumstances, if any, will delay a charge-off, and when the bank recognizes losses (i.e., daily, weekly, or monthly).

(f) Request a report detailing closed-end accounts more than 120 days past due and open-end accounts more than 180 days past due that have not been charged off or, if secured, written down to the value of collateral, less cost to sell. Review the report with management, and determine why those balances remain on the bank's books and whether there are system or policy issues that need to be corrected.

4. Evaluate the adequacy of the bank's policies and practices for payment posting and assessing late fees.

(a) Review the payment posting procedures and practices and determine if payments are promptly posted.

(b) Determine the conditions under which late fees are imposed[16] and, if applicable, at what point the fees are suspended.

---

[16] 12 CFR 227.15 (Regulation AA) indicates it is an unfair practice for a bank to assess a late fee when the only delinquency is attributable to the late fee assessed on an earlier installment, and the

(c) Determine the bank's policy for collecting late fees (e.g., as part of the next regularly scheduled payment) and how unpaid late fees are accounted for, tracked, and collected.

(d) Determine whether the bank's process for evaluating the ramifications of changes in late fee policies, including dollar amounts and grace periods, is adequate prior to broad implementation.

(e) Assess whether the available MIS and reports provide the information necessary to evaluate the effect of late fees. Specifically, assess whether the information is sufficient to allow management to determine whether the fees have the desired effect on performance (i.e., improve on-time payments), whether late fees result in negative amortization, and the extent to which late fees assessed are actually collected.

(f) Ensure that the bank has established adequate loss allowance for accrued but uncollectible interest and fees, including late fees, in either the allowance or a separate reserve.

5. Assess the appropriateness of management's collection strategies.

(a) Through discussions with management, determine how management develops collection strategies, who is responsible, and how the success of the strategies is measured.

(b) Determine what triggers strategy changes, and who has authority to direct revisions.

(c) Establish whether the bank uses scoring or any other predictive techniques to assist in the collection of accounts. If so, determine:

– The scores or techniques used, how they are used, and whether they are internally or externally developed.

– When the scores or techniques were last validated, by whom, and the results of the validation.

6. If applicable, assess the adequacy of the bank's use of champion/challenger strategies.

(a) Identify the person or group responsible for strategy development.

---

payment is otherwise a full payment for the applicable period and is paid on its due date or within an applicable grace period.

(b) Determine that the development process begins with a clear identification of strategy objectives and relies on reasonable assumptions and complete and accurate MIS.

(c) Determine that the bank's controls provide for proper testing (i.e., test size, time frame, and account population and characteristics) of challenger strategies prior to making decisions to expand challenger penetration or to replace the existing champion strategy.

(d) Assess the monitoring process and determine whether the bank accumulates and analyzes appropriate data to measure strategy success.

(e) Determine that the bank maintains adequate documentation of the various strategies.

7.   Determine whether the bank uses cure programs such as re-aging, extensions, deferrals, renewals, rewrites, fixed payments, internal or external workout programs (e.g., Consumer Credit Counseling Services (CCCS)), or settlement/forgiveness programs. If so:

(a) Assess the adequacy of the policies and procedures used to administer the programs and compliance with the OCC 2000-20, "Uniform Retail Credit Classification Policy and Account Management Policy," and OCC 2003-1, "Account Management and Loss Allowance Guidance" regarding limits, analysis, documentation, amortization periods, and allowance considerations.

(b) Review and evaluate any test and analysis summaries completed prior to the implementation of new cure programs.

(c) Determine whether the bank's programs appropriately address proper income recognition for restructured loans.

(d) Evaluate the MIS and reporting used to monitor and analyze the performance of each program. Compare performance with forecasts and bank objectives and tolerances. In addition to reports listed in procedure 10(b), ensure that management generates and reviews reports detailing:
   – Volume (balance and unit) trends for cure program accounts, by product, program, vintage, and in total.
   – Loss performance, by product, program, vintage, and in total.

- Performance of the accounts 30, 90, 180, 270, 360, etc., days subsequent to the cure.

- Performance of accounts cured more than once, broken down by the number of times cured and tracked over time.

- Policy exceptions and the performance of those exceptions.

(e) Compare the performance of accounts in cure programs with the performance of those in the general retail product population using performance measures in (d).

(f) Assess the current and potential impact of such programs on the bank's reported performance (asset quality) and profitability, including allowance and capital implications.

Note: If management accepts external debt management plans, such as CCCS, management should be able to monitor the performance of accounts by individual credit counseling agency.

8. Review the bank's "skip tracing" practices and procedures to track delinquent customers and determine their effectiveness.

(a) Ascertain what portion of the portfolio lacks current/correct telephone numbers and mailing addresses.

(b) Evaluate the adequacy of the bank's process for obtaining missing contact information.

(c) Determine whether the bank has a process to exclude accounts without pertinent contact information from promotional initiatives and favorable account management treatment.

(d) If applicable, determine whether the bank appropriately monitors outside agencies used to skip trace accounts.

(e) Determine whether skip accounts are flagged for accelerated charge-off if attempts to locate borrower are unsuccessful.

9. Assess whether the bank's automated systems for collecting delinquent accounts are adequate and discuss these systems with management.

(a) Determine which technologies and processes the bank uses to collect accounts (e.g., automated dialers, collection letters, statement messaging, and videos), how each is used, and the key reports generated to monitor performance. With respect to the latter, determine whether the reports provide sufficient data to allow management to make appropriate decisions.

(b) If auto-dialing is used, determine how the system routes "no contact" accounts, or accounts that collectors remove from the dialer because of a promise to pay or a payment arrangement.

(c) Determine whether the systems generate a sufficient audit trail.

(d) Determine whether managers, supervisors, and quality control staff have the ability to listen to collector phone calls on-line.

(e) Evaluate the adequacy of the bank's contingency plans, and determine whether the plans are tested regularly.

10. Assess the quality, accuracy, and completeness of MIS reports and other analyses used to manage the collections process. Specifically:

(a) Evaluate the quality of MIS collection reports regularly provided to executive management, and determine whether the reports provide adequate information, including comparisons with collection objectives and tolerances, for timely decision-making.

(b) Determine the appropriateness and accuracy of key collection reports. Review specifically:
   – Vintage and coincident delinquency and loss reports.

   – Roll-rate reports and migration-to-loss reports.

   – Cure program reports, in total, by program, and by collector, including reports that track the volume (number and dollar) of accounts entering cure programs, accounts awaiting re-age or extension, and the actual performance of accounts in the various programs.

   – Collector and strategy or special handling queue reports.

   – Productivity reports, including information such as call penetration, right party contact, promises made and kept, dollars collected, and staffing summaries.

   Note: If not removed, insufficient funds checks (NSF) can affect several of the metrics above. Management should have a method to identify, if not correct, the effects of NSF checks on the metrics.

(c) Determine whether customer service or department other than collections can initiate collection activities, such as cure programs.

If so, determine whether appropriate monitoring MIS are in place to monitor volumes and credit performance of accounts in collection activities initiated outside collections.

11. Evaluate the adequacy of the bank's policies and procedures for foreclosure and repossession, and for the disposition of collateral.

(a) Determine the point at which foreclosure or repossession processes are initiated.

(b) Determine that policies and procedures provide for timely disposition of collateral and maximize liquidation values.

(c) Evaluate the adequacy of the bank's accounting for foreclosed and repossessed assets; specifically, determine that:
   – Foreclosed or repossessed assets are appropriately transferred from loans to other real estate owned or repossessed assets at the lower of book or fair market value less cost to sell. *Note: Real estate should be transferred to other real estate owned once the bank gains effective control of or title to the property.*

   – Assets are routinely evaluated for impairment, and that impaired values are charged off each quarter-end, at a minimum.

   – Management routinely reviews inventory aging reports and takes appropriate action on stale inventory (e.g., other real estate owned longer than one year, repossessed assets in the bank's possession longer than 90 days).

12. Determine what system(s) the bank uses to recover charged-off accounts and deficiency balances and whether they interface with the bank's collection management system(s). If not, determine how the recovery unit gathers and uses information about prior collection activities.

13. Determine whether the bank uses outside agencies (including attorneys and attorney networks) to collect delinquent accounts or to recover losses. If so:

(a) Assess the bank's due diligence process for selecting vendors.

(b) Determine whether the bank's legal counsel and compliance officer have reviewed the contracts with and practices of third-party collectors.

(c) Evaluate any forward-flow contracts to collection agencies, including performance tolerances and termination requirements (important for remediation or severing the contract if poor performance). *Note: Forward-flow contracts provide agencies a set number of accounts at a determined frequency and assist the bank in forecasting placements.*

(d) Determine the frequency and method of rotating accounts, including reasons supporting the method, between collection and recovery agencies and in-house collections, i.e., distinctions between primary, secondary, and tertiary.

(e) Review productivity and cost reports for each vendor, and discuss with management how the bank monitors the success of third-party collectors and places work load accordingly.

(f) Evaluate the systems and controls used to supervise out-placed accounts, including active reconcilements of amounts collected and fees disbursed to each vendor.

(g) Review MIS used to monitor the performance of outside agencies.

(h) Evaluate the adequacy and frequency of the bank's audits (on-site and modem, if applicable) of third-party collectors.

Note: See the "Third-Party Management" in the "Supplemental Examination Procedures" for additional guidance on reviewing third-party relationships.

14. Assess the bank's recovery performance using historical results and industry averages, by product, as guidelines.

(a) Determine whether the bank periodically sells charged-off accounts. If so, determine the reasonableness of forecasts.

(b) Evaluate the bank's recoveries in light of prior period losses.

(c) Evaluate the accuracy of the recovery figures. If the bank charges accrued but uncollected interest and fees against income rather than the allowance, verify that recoveries are reported accordingly (i.e., include principal only). Refer to appendix D, "Account Management and Loss Allowance Guidance Checklist."

(d) Assess the costs associated with the dollars recovered, and explore trends.

15. Assess the appropriateness of the bank's fraud policies and procedures.

 (a) Review the bank's definition of fraud losses and ensure that it is reasonable and appropriately distinguishes fraud from credit losses.

 (b) Ascertain compliance with the charge-off requirements of OCC 2000-20, "Uniform Retail Credit Classification and Account Management Policy" (90 days from discovery).

 (c) Confirm that fraud losses are recognized as operating expenses rather than charges to the allowance for loan and lease losses.

 (d) Ensure that the bank's policies differentiate between amounts in an account alleged to be fraudulent and undisputed amounts. For example, for open-end credit, some banks may re-age the entire amount owed to current pending the outcome of the fraud investigation when that treatment should not extend to undisputed amounts.

 (e) If the investigation negates the fraud allegation, verify that the bank returns accounts to the previous delinquency status and immediately reinstates collection efforts.

 Note: When an account is reported as fraudulent, the reason should be given (either because account activity is alleged to be fraudulent, because it is confirmed to be fraudulent, or because the application is fraudulent). An account that has had an NSF check or that did not make the first payment should not automatically be identified as fraudulent.

16. Review the adequacy of MIS reports pertaining to fraud.

 (a) Determine whether the information is sufficient to monitor fraud and the effectiveness of fraud controls, including the appropriate filing of suspicious activity reports (SARs).

 (b) Assess the levels and trends of fraud losses, by product, compared with industry averages and discuss any atypical findings with management. *Note: Fraud losses are often depicted as fraud losses divided by sales.*

17. Assess the adequacy of internal and external audit, quality assurance, loan review, and risk management in the collections area, including scope, frequency, timing, report content, and independence.

(a) Review relevant audit, quality assurance, loan review, and risk management reports.

(b) Determine the adequacy and timeliness of management's responses to the issues identified and any findings or issues requiring follow-up. If warranted based on the significance of the issue or concerns about the adequacy of the response or action taken, test corrective action.

18. Conduct transaction testing to verify your initial conclusions with respect to the bank's collection programs and activities. In addition to determining adherence to approved policies and procedures, determine whether the programs and activities result in an enduring positive change in credit risk or provide temporary relief. Verify that MIS reports accurately capture the activities and the subsequent performance of the accounts (referring to the appendix A, "Transaction Testing," for additional guidance).

(a) Sample accounts that were at least 60 days delinquent in the month preceding the examination and are now current to determine whether the customer cured the delinquency or whether the account was cured artificially (e.g., re-age or extension). If the latter, determine whether the action was consistent with existing bank policy, and that it complied with OCC 2000-20, "Uniform Retail Credit Classification and Account Management Policy."

(b) Sample accounts from each of the primary collection areas (e.g., early-stage, late-stage, skip, bankruptcy) to determine adherence to policy. The sample helps an examiner understand the collection process and strategies employed. *Note: This sample is often best completed or supplemented by sitting with collectors as they work accounts.*

(c) Sample loans from **each** of the following areas to assess compliance with the bank policies for the programs and reasonableness of decisions: recent re-ages, workouts, extensions, deferrals, renewals, modifications, or rewrites. Decisions should also be compared with the bank's normal underwriting guidelines with respect to loan-to-value, amortization period, debt or repayment limitations, and pricing.

(d) Sample charged-off accounts and review all activities that occurred prior to charge-off to determine whether the bank employs practices that result in loss deferral.

(e) Sample identified fraud accounts and review all activities to determine propriety of practices, adherence to policy, and timeliness of charge-off practices.

19. Develop conclusions with respect to the effectiveness of the collection function, including the collection strategies and programs employed, and the implications for the quality of the portfolio and the quantity and direction of credit risk.

Open-End Credit (Credit Card, Personal, and Home Equity Lines)

20. Determine the delinquency level at which the bank temporarily suspends lines of credit and the level at which it permanently closes an account. Also:

(a) Determine whether scoring models or other methods contribute to decisions to permanently close lines of credit.

(b) Evaluate the circumstances under which a closed account can be reactivated, and verify that the collections department refers such accounts to the credit department for an underwriting decision.

21. Ascertain whether the bank's collection strategies include the use of default pricing (also known as penalty pricing). If so:

(a) Determine the performance criteria used to trigger higher pricing, and the conditions that will return accounts to lower pricing.

(b) Assess management's objectives for imposing such a strategy and the quality of the supporting analysis. Be particularly alert to whether the analysis adequately considers the possible ramifications of the strategy, including reputation risk, negative retention, increased credit losses, and decreased interest income in the long term.

(c) Determine that the strategy was properly tested using reasonable sample sizes and time frames, and that the initial performance assumptions were adequately validated prior to full rollout.

(d) Determine management's performance targets for the default pricing strategy, and review actual performance against those metrics.

(e) Evaluate the adequacy of the MIS and reporting used to monitor the performance of accounts during and subsequent to default pricing.

(f) Assess the timeliness and appropriateness of management's response to negative strategy results.

Vehicle Loans and Leases

22. Assess repossession activity and performance, including the timeliness and appropriateness of repossession charge-offs and disposal, ensuring that management is aware of any third parties, including subcontractors, used during the process.

    (a) Assess the bank's method of valuing repossessed assets, and determine whether repossessions are written down to fair value at the time of repossession or upon sale. If the latter, ensure that sales occur promptly and that the value of the asset is adequately adjusted in the interim for repossessions with protracted selling periods.

    (b) Evaluate how the bank disposes of repossessed assets. Focus on arrangements with local dealers, auction houses, and public or private sales, and how well management times the sales and balances inventory allocation with the various vendors.

    (c) Review repossession volumes and trends, including repossession rate (number of repossessions per 1,000 accounts), partial and full balance loss per repossession, and average time to disposal. For large automobile lenders, performance differences may be noted by geographic area, make, and model.

23. For leasing, review the accounts receivable aging for end-of-term fees, including excess mileage, wear and tear, and termination or disposition fees. Determine the level of the bank's success with collecting these fees, and assess the need to write off uncollectible receivables if the fees are recognized on an accrual basis. Many lessors recognize fees on a cash basis.

24. Determine how management reviews vehicle residuals for other than temporary impairment per the requirements of FAS 13, Accounting for Leases. Verify that bank management expenses other than temporary residual impairment (writes the residual down to the anticipated residual value).

25. Review management's residual realization reports.[17] For those segments with consistent residual realization rates less than 100 percent, determine the effectiveness of bank management's procedures for recognizing other than temporary impairment of residuals. Direct bank management to recognize other than temporary residual impairment, if appropriate.

26. Determine whether the bank offers extensions to its lease customers. If so, determine how management quantifies, analyzes, and tracks other than temporary impairment for this segment of the portfolio. *Note: Extending the term of the lease through payment extensions creates additional risk of loss due to additional vehicle depreciation.*

27. Review the matured lease report and identify leases where the lessee has failed to return the vehicle. Review the adequacy of the bank's procedures for charging off these balances as uncollectible.

Off-Lease Vehicle Remarketing

28. Assess how well the bank manages and reports on leases that have run their full term.

   (a) Discuss with bank management their vehicle remarketing methods (e.g., direct retail, auction, dealer consignment, and wholesalers).

   (b) Review and discuss scheduled run-off reports to identify concentrations (e.g., lease maturities, vehicle types, manufacturers, models, and geographic location).

   (c) Determine the appropriateness of staffing levels based upon the marketing method and projected turn-in volume.

   (d) Review past and present turn-in volume and management's projections for next year.

   (e) Assess the effectiveness of strategies used prior to lease termination to minimize turn-ins (e.g., settlement offers and lease-to-loan or lease-to-lease products).

---

[17] Residual realization reports detail profitability by items such as lease term, make, model, and model year. Residual realization equals the net cash received from the sale of the vehicle divided by the booked residual value and expressed as a percentage.

(f) Determine whether the bank's systems can analyze the costs and benefits of moving vehicles to different geographic areas to maximize sales value.

(g) Review bank management's procedures for charging off balances in excess of the net realizable value.

29. Review and assess the adequacy of management reports used to determine the effectiveness of the remarketing process. Reports should include:

- The average loss or gain on remarketed vehicles in total and by vehicle segment.

- The average loss or gain on remarketed vehicles by original term.

- Comparisons of amounts received at sale versus average guidebook value.

- Return rates in total, by lease term, and by vehicle type, make, and model.

- Off-lease inventory aging reports.

- Sales reports for sold inventory.

- Matured lease reports where the lessee has failed to return the vehicle.

- Comparison of actual results and metrics with the bank's objectives and tolerances for remarketing.

Risk Management and Control Functions

Objective: Evaluate the adequacy of the bank's processes for identifying, measuring, monitoring, and controlling risk by reviewing the effectiveness of risk management and other control functions.

Note: If the bank uses affiliates or third-party vendors for loan acquisition, servicing, control, or other key functions, refer to "Third-Party Management" in "Supplemental Examination Procedures."

1.   Assess the structure,[18] management, and staffing of each of the control functions, including risk management, loan review, internal and external audit, quality assurance, and compliance review.

Note: Compliance is clearly a significant risk for retail credit. While consumer compliance examiners generally assess the quality of the compliance review function, safety and soundness examiners should understand compliance-related roles, responsibilities, and coverage, as well as how compliance controls fit into the overall control plan.

2.   Ascertain the roles and responsibilities and reporting lines of the various control functions through discussions with senior management.

(a) Review the organization chart for each function, and evaluate the quality and depth of staff (including number of positions) based on the assigned role and the size and complexity of the operation:
    – Review the experience levels of senior managers and staff.

    – Determine whether employees are capable of evaluating the line of business activities.

    – Review management and staff turnover levels.

(b) Discuss the structure and staffing plans, including known or anticipated gaps or vacancies, with senior management.

(c) Review compensation plans to determine that performance measurements are appropriately targeted to risk identification and control objectives.

(d) Determine whether organizational reporting lines create the necessary level of independence.

Note: If the management and staff of a control function lack the knowledge or capability to adequately review all or parts of retail operations, management may need to consult or hire appropriate outside expertise.

3.   Discuss with senior managers how they ensure that significant risks are appropriately monitored by at least one control function, and how they assess the effectiveness of each function.

---

[18] Depending on the bank, risk management functions may be managed from different areas in the bank (i.e., some from the line of business and others from the corporate offices).

4. Determine whether the risk management function appropriately monitors, analyzes, and controls the bank's credit risk.

   (a) Determine risk management's recurring responsibilities and major projects, including status of projects, and assess the adequacy of those activities in light of the bank's retail credit risk profile, the products offered, and the complexity of the operation.

   (b) Determine whether credit risk decisions involve all key functional areas, including risk management, marketing, finance, operations, compliance, legal, and information technology, either formally or informally.

   (c) Determine whether risk management is involved in tactical credit decisions, such as credit program approvals, program renewals, new products, marketing campaigns, and annual financial planning.

   (d) Obtain descriptions of key management reports to determine the types and purposes of reports produced, report distribution, and frequency of preparation.

   (e) Obtain a sample of recent ad hoc or special studies or board reports produced by risk management to determine the types of analyses performed, the reasonableness of the scopes and methodologies used, and the accuracy of the conclusions drawn, including the adequacy of the support provided.

   (f) Determine what technologies and risk tools are deployed and risk management's role in the management of those tools, including data warehouse, portfolio management software, credit scoring and adaptive control systems, and risk models.

   (g) Determine whether market, competitive, legislative, and other external factors are considered in the risk management process.

5. Determine if management considers consumer complaints and complaint resolution in the risk management process. If not previously completed, obtain copies of the OCC (complaints reported to the Customer Assistance Group) and bank consumer complaint logs. Evaluate the information for significant issues and trends. *Note: Complaints serve as a valuable early warning indicator for compliance, credit, and operational issues, including discriminatory unfair, deceptive, abusive, and predatory practices.*

---

6. Determine whether changes to practices and products, including new products and practices, are fully tested, analyzed, and supported prior to broad implementation. *Note: See "Marketing and Product Development" in "Supplemental Examination Procedures" for testing guidelines.*

7. Test the effectiveness of the bank's risk management process for existing and new products, marketing and collection initiatives, and changes to risk tolerance (e.g., initiating or changing credit criteria or adopting new scoring systems/technologies). Select at least one significant new product, account management practice (e.g., line increase, pricing, payment holiday), or collections initiative (e.g., workout program, rewrite) and track it through all facets of the management process.

   (a) Planning. If tracking a new loan product, for example, determine how the bank developed new underwriting standards (e.g., how did it analyze the applicability of the underwriting criteria and marketing strategies then in use and what was the basis of any projections), and how did it derive new criteria or strategies (e.g., what were the key drivers for credit, revenue).

   (b) Execution. Evaluate the adequacy of the process employed to ensure that new criteria and changes were implemented as intended. *Note: This component is generally performed by some combination of information technology staff, product management, quality control, audit, and loan operations.*

   (c) Measurement. Ascertain how adherence to standards is measured and how management measures impact using back-end monitoring and analysis. Determine the key measurements management uses to analyze the effectiveness of its decisions (e.g., responder analyses, first or early payment default, vintage reporting for delinquencies and losses, activation/booking, utilization, risk-adjusted margin, profit and loss), and the adequacy of back-testing analyses (comparison to targets, identification and analysis of anomalies).

   (d) Adjustment. Determine how feedback results (lessons learned, opportunities identified) are incorporated into the process as course corrections or adjustments. Assess the process for making adjustments as problems or unexpected performance results are identified, and whether the process is both timely and appropriate.

8. Determine whether the bank has the data warehousing capabilities (i.e., the capacity to store and retrieve pertinent data) to support necessary monitoring, analytical, and forecasting activities.

9. Evaluate executive management's monthly and quarterly report packages. Specifically:

   (a) Determine whether the reports accurately and completely describe the state of the bank's retail lending.

   (b) Evaluate whether reports adequately measure credit risk (e.g., score distributions and vintage reports), identify trends, describe significant variances, and present issues. *Note: Reports should allow management to assess whether retail operations remain consistent with strategic objectives and within established risk, return, and credit performance tolerances.*

   (c) Determine whether reports clearly evidence analysis of performance results and trends rather than merely depict data.

10. Obtain feedback from other examiners assigned to the retail credit examination regarding the adequacy of reports available.

Credit Scoring Models

Note: Refer to OCC bulletins 97-24, "Credit Scoring Models, Examiner Guidance" and 2000-16, "Risk Modeling, Model Validation" for additional background and guidance in this area.

11. Assess the scorecard management process, and determine the department or personnel responsible for scorecard and model development or procurement, implementation, including monitoring, and validation.

   (a) Obtain a model inventory to determine the models in use. The inventory should include:

   – Name of the model.

   – Model description.

   – Type (custom, generic, behavioral).

- Date developed.

- Source (name of the vendor or in-house modeler).

- Purpose (e.g., application, response, attrition, pricing, profitability).

- Date last validated and next scheduled validation date.

- Models under development, if any.

- Management contact for each model.

(b) Determine whether scorecards are used for purposes consistent with the development process/populations. If not (e.g., applied to a different product or new geographic area), assess the ramifications and acceptability.

(c) Review the most recent independent validation reports for key risk models, and discuss the conclusions with risk management.

(d) Discuss how management uses the models to target prospects, underwrite applications, and manage the portfolio.

(e) Determine how management measures the ongoing performance and robustness of models (e.g., good/bad separation, bad rate analysis, and maximum delinquency ("ever bad") distribution reports).

(f) Review scorecard tracking reports to determine how well the models are performing. Select tracking reports for key models and determine whether model performance is stable or deteriorating, and how management compensates for deteriorating efficacy.

(g) Determine how cutoffs are established, reviewed, and adjusted. Review the most recent cutoff analysis for key risk models.

(h) Determine the bank's score override policy, assess the adequacy of associated tracking, and review override volume and performance. Determine whether management segments low-side overrides by reason and tracks delinquencies or defaults by reason and override score bands, and assess the performance and trends.

(i) Review chronology logs to determine changes in the credit criteria or risk profile and to explain shifts in the portfolio, including volume and performance.

12. Select at least one key credit risk scoring model and fully assess the adequacy of the model management process:

(a) Review the original model documentation or scorecard manual, and assess management's adherence to the modeler's recommended scorecard maintenance routine.

(b) Compare the population characteristics and the developmental sample performance odds with the bank's current experience.

(c) Review model performance reports and assess the adequacy of management's response to the issues or trends identified. Reports reviewed may include applicant distribution, population stability, characteristic analysis (if indicated by a population shift), override tracking, and vintage delinquency and loss distribution reports.

Loan Review

13. Assess the adequacy of the loan review process for retail lending. Determine whether:

(a) Loan review's scope includes providing a risk assessment of the quality of risk management and quantity of risk for retail lending in aggregate and by lines of business.

(b) The scope includes appropriate testing for adherence to key credit policies and procedures.

(c) The scope includes appropriate reviews to assess compliance with applicable laws, regulations, and guidance, including assessing whether any lending practices are discriminatory, unfair, deceptive, abusive, and predatory.

(d) The scope includes a review of the accuracy and adequacy of MIS reporting.

(e) The frequency of reviews is acceptable based on the significance of the risks involved.

(f) Staffing levels and experience are commensurate with the complexity and risk in the retail lending area.

(g) Loan review is independent from the production process.

(h) Loan review possesses sufficient authority and influence to correct deficiencies or curb dangerous practices.

14. Review recent loan review reports for retail lending. Determine whether:

- Reports are issued in a timely manner following completion of the on-site work.

- Reports provide meaningful conclusions and accurately identify concerns.

- Significant issues require management's written response.

- Management initiates timely and appropriate corrective action.

- Issues identified and the status of corrective actions are tracked and reported to senior management.

Note: Weaknesses identified by examiners, but not identified by the loan review, may be evidence of deficiencies in loan review processes or staffing.

Quality Control

15. Assess the adequacy of quality control process for retail lending. Determine whether:

(a) The process assesses ongoing compliance with key credit and operational policies and procedures, and applicable laws and regulations for all primary areas, including:
    - Loan origination.

    - Account management programs.

    - Fraud.

    - Customer service.

    - Collections.

    Note: Quality control processes should be established for all direct lending activities and any third-party loan servicing and origination arrangements.

(b) Quality control tests the integrity and accuracy of MIS data for areas listed in (a).

(c) The frequency of reviews is properly geared to the significance of the risk.

(d) The testing/sample sizes are appropriate.

(e) The quality control function possesses sufficient authority and influence to correct deficiencies or curb dangerous practices.

16. Review a sample of quality assurance ongoing testing worksheets and periodic summary reports (e.g., monthly summaries of testing conclusions). Determine whether:

- Reporting process allows for timely feedback to management.

- Worksheets and summary reports accurately identify concerns.

- Significant issues require management's written response.

- Management initiates timely and appropriate corrective action.

- Issues identified and the status of corrective actions are tracked and reported to senior management.

Note: Weaknesses identified by examiners, but not identified by the quality control function, may be evidence of deficiencies in quality control processes or staffing.

17. If the quality assurance function is not independent from the loan production process, determine whether internal audit or loan review tests quality assurance to ensure that management can rely on those findings.

18. If reviews and testing by the quality control area do not include significant risk areas, communicate findings to the examiner-in-charge to determine whether it is appropriate to complete transactional testing in areas not covered by quality control.

Internal Audit

19. Assess the adequacy of internal audit for retail lending. Determine whether:

   (a) The scope includes appropriate testing for adherence to key credit and operational policies and procedures.

   (b) The frequency of reviews is properly geared to the significance of the risks.

   (c) Internal audit is independent.

   (d) Internal audit possesses sufficient authority and influence to correct deficiencies or curb dangerous practices.

Note: Refer to the "Internal and External Audits" booklet of the Comptroller's Handbook for additional information.

20. Review recent internal audit reports for retail lending. Determine whether:

- Reports are issued in a timely manner following completion of the on-site work.

- Reports accurately identify concerns.

- Significant issues require management's written response.

- Management initiates timely and appropriate corrective action.

- Issues identified and the status of corrective actions are tracked and reported to senior management.

Note: Weaknesses identified by examiner, but not identified by internal audit, may be evidence of deficiencies in internal audit processes or staffing

Other Controls

21. Confirm that there is an adequate process in place to reconcile major balance sheet categories and general ledger entries on a daily basis.

22. Identify and determine the adequacy of the bank's process for regularly evaluating data integrity and MIS accuracy.

   (a) Review the scope and frequency of internal audit or other reviews of MIS accuracy.

   (b) Review the findings of the most recent reviews.

23. Develop conclusions with respect to the adequacy of the bank's processes for identifying, measuring, monitoring, and controlling risk by reviewing the effectiveness of risk management and other control functions. Clearly document all findings.

Profitability

Objective: Assess the quantity, quality, and sustainability of retail credit earnings.

Note: For banks that securitize, examiners should also review income statements for managed assets.

1. Obtain and review copies of the income statement for the retail credit portfolio and for each significant product. Ensure that the reports are "fully loaded," i.e., that they include all pertinent income and expense items including overhead and funding costs.

2. Ascertain the contribution of the retail credit portfolio to corporate earnings, and the expected contribution in the future.

    (a) Review executive management monthly and/or quarterly performance reports and portfolio quality MIS packages.

    (b) Review historical trends, including changes in the product contributions.

    (c) Review financial projections and budget and plan variances.

    (d) Review significant income and expense components and measures. Items reviewed should include noninterest income (fees and other add-ons), marketing expense, charge-offs, net interest margin, and risk-adjusted yield.

    (e) Evaluate the methodologies, assumptions, and documentary support for the bank's planning and forecasting processes. Determine whether material changes are expected in any of the key income and expense components and measures.

    (f) Determine management's return on assets (ROA), return on managed assets (ROMA), and return on equity (ROE) hurdles, and the actual returns as of the examination date. *Note: Asset-based measures are typically more meaningful for comparison because banks allocate capital differently.*

3. Verify that the bank appropriately recognizes uncollectible accrued interest and fees through the allowance for loan and lease losses,

---

through a separate interest and fee reserve, or through cash income recognition.

4. Review the bank's stress test and discuss potential earnings volatility through an economic cycle with management in order to assess sustainability. If the bank does not perform stress testing, discuss if and how management prices loans to withstand economic downturns.

5. Determine whether the bank's cost accounting system is capable of generating profit data by product, segment (including grade), channel, and account.

6. Assess the profitability of each retail credit product:

   (a) For each product, review profitability by credit score band, credit grade, sub-portfolio (e.g., unsecured vs. secured credit card), segment (e.g., loan-to-value differences), and vintage, as appropriate.

   (b) Compare actual results with projections and discuss variances with management.

7. Evaluate profitability by channel.

   (a) Through discussions with the examiner responsible for third-party management, determine profitability generated through the various channels (e.g., dealers, brokers, and third-party originators).

   (b) Compare the profitability of the loans generated by the various channels.

8. Determine the adequacy of the pricing method.

   (a) Review the pricing strategy, pricing method, and pricing model, if applicable.

   (b) Review the major assumptions used in the pricing method and assess reasonableness. Be alert to differences in assumptions by product and channel.

   (c) Determine whether pricing is driven by risk, capital, or some other allocation method or hurdle, and how much, if any, it is driven by the competition.

(d) Determine whether the pricing method incorporates a realistic break-even analysis, and whether the analysis reflects the true costs of premature account closures (attrition) and reductions (prepayment).

(e) Review the pricing matrix, by product.

9. Assess the adequacy of planning, reporting, and analysis with respect to attrition and prepayment. Specifically, ascertain whether management identifies the volume and trends of accounts with high interest rates relative to market or low introductory rates to determine exposure and impact on earnings.

10. Develop conclusions with respect to the quantity, quality, and sustainability of retail credit earnings.

Third-Party Management

Objective: Determine the extent of third-party involvement in retail lending activities and evaluate the effectiveness of management's third-party oversight and risk management processes.

Note: These procedures apply to any arrangements with third parties to provide retail credit-related services to customers on the bank's behalf. Banks may fully "outsource" loan originations (using brokers, dealers, or telemarketers, for example), collection activities (using collection agencies or attorneys), or the offering of products (debit and credit cards, for example) in the bank's name.

The terms "third party," "third-party vendors," and "vendors" are used interchangeably throughout the following procedures. "Vendor management" is the term used to describe the bank's process for overseeing these parties. Refer to OCC Bulletin 2001-47, "Third-Party Relationships, Risk Management Principles"; OCC Bulletin 2002-16, "Bank Use of Foreign-Based Third-Party Service Providers, Risk Management Guidance"; and Advisory Letter 2000-9, "Third-Party Risk" for additional information on OCC expectations.

1. Determine the adequacy of the bank's third-party vendor management program.

(a) Assess the adequacy of the vendor management policy, and determine that analysis, documentation, and reporting requirements are clearly addressed.

(b) Determine that management has designated an individual to be responsible for the program, and delegated the authority necessary for its effective administration to that individual.

(c) Review the bank's process for maintaining a complete list of third-party vendors used by the bank.

(d) Review the bank's criteria for designating "significant" vendors according to the dollar amount of the contract, the importance of the service provided, and the potential risk involved in the activity.

Note: While the vendor management program should address all vendor relationships, the OCC expects a more rigorous process to manage those vendors deemed significant.

(e) Review the bank's due diligence process and ensure the process:
   - Provides for comprehensive, well-documented reviews by qualified staff.

   - Identifies any potential conflicts of interest with bank directors, officers, staff, and their related interests.

   - Addresses compliance with all applicable laws and regulations, including safety and soundness regulatory standards, and laws prohibiting lending discrimination and unfair or deceptive practices.

2. Identify vendors that provide significant retail credit services on the bank's behalf, particularly those that provide loan origination, servicing, or complete products. Determine the bank's relationship manager for each of those vendors.

3. Verify that bank management's expertise in the outsourced activities is sufficient to accurately identify and manage the risks involved.

4. Determine whether management has adequate controls, including policies and procedures and monitoring controls, to avoid becoming involved with a third party engaged in discriminatory, unfair, deceptive, abusive and predatory lending practices. Policies and procedures should address, if applicable, the circumstances in which

the bank may make loans involving features or actions that have been associated with discriminatory, unfair, deceptive, abusive, and predatory lending practices, including:

- Lending predominantly on the liquidation value of collateral rather than the borrower's ability to service the debt.

- Refinancing loans frequently.

- Refinancing special subsidized mortgages that contain terms favorable to the borrower.

- Requiring single-premium life insurance or similar products.

- Using negative amortization.

- Requiring balloon payments in short-term transactions.

- Charging prepayment penalties in the later years of a loan.

- Charging high financing points, fees, or penalties.

- Increasing interest rate increases upon default.

- Inserting mandatory arbitration clauses.

- Making high-cost loans (e.g., loans subject to the Home Ownership and Equity Protection Act).

If weaknesses or concerns are found, consult the bank's EIC or compliance examiner.

Note: For additional information refer to the Comptroller's Handbook, "Fair Lending" booklet, and OCC advisory letters 2002-3, "Guidance on Unfair or Deceptive Acts or Practices"; 2003-2, "Guidelines for National Banks to Guard Against Predatory and Abusive Lending Practices"; 2003-3 "Avoiding Predatory and Abusive Lending Practices in Brokered and Purchased Loans"; 2004-4, "Secured Credit Cards"; and 2004-10, "Credit Card Practices."

5.   Assess the adequacy of contract management, focusing on the process for ensuring that clauses necessary to effectively manage the vendor are included.

   (a) Ensure that the bank has a current contract on file for all third-party vendors and that the bank monitors key dates (e.g., maturity, renewal, adjustment periods).

(b) Review a sample of contracts with significant vendors to ensure that the contracts satisfactorily address:

- The scope of the arrangement, including the frequency, content, and format of services provided by each party.

- Outsourcing notifications or approvals required, if the vendor proposes to subcontract a service to another party.

- All costs and compensation, including any incentives.

- Performance standards, including when and if standards can be adjusted, and the consequences of failing to meet those standards.

- Reporting and MIS requirements.

- Data ownership and access.

- Appropriate privacy and confidentiality restrictions.

- Requirements for compliance with all applicable laws and regulations, including safety and soundness regulatory standards, and laws prohibiting lending discrimination and unfair or deceptive practices.

- Where brokers and dealers are used in the loan origination process, requirements that the brokers and dealers make best efforts to ensure that the loans offered to borrowers are consistent with their needs, objectives, and financial situation.

- Mandatory vendor control functions such as quality assurance and audit, including requirements for submitting audit results to the bank.

- Expectations and responsibilities for business resumption and contingency plans.

- Responsibility for consumer complaint resolution and associated reporting to the bank.

- Vendor financial statement submission requirements.

- Appropriate dispute resolution, liability, recourse, penalty, indemnification, and termination clauses.

- The authority for the bank to perform on-site vendor reviews. *Note: Third-party performance of services is also subject to OCC examination oversight if warranted.*

(c) Determine whether the bank's monitoring of vendors' adherence to their contracts (especially to financial terms and performance standards) is adequate in frequency and scope.

(d) Determine whether issues identified through the monitoring process are appropriately resolved in a timely manner.

6. Assess the adequacy of the monitoring process for significant vendors.

(a) Using the sample of significant vendors reviewed in procedure 5(b), confirm that the bank's oversight incorporates, at a minimum:
    - Reports evidencing the third party's performance relative to service level agreements and other contract provisions.

    - Customer complaints and resolutions for the services and products outsourced.

    - Third-party financial statements and audit reports.

    - Compliance with applicable laws and regulations.

(b) Evaluate whether the process results in an accurate determination of whether contractual terms and conditions are being met, and whether any revisions to service-level agreements or other terms are needed.

(c) Verify whether management documents and follows up on performance, operational, or compliance problems and whether the documentation and follow-ups are timely and effective.

(d) Determine whether the relationship manager or other bank staff periodically meets with its vendors to discuss performance and operational issues.

(e) Determine whether vendor management administers call monitoring, mystery shopper, customer call back, or customer satisfaction programs, if appropriate.

(f) Assess the adequacy of the bank's process for determining when on-site reviews are warranted, the scope of those reviews, and reporting of results.

(g) Determine whether management evaluates the third party's ongoing ability to perform the contracted functions in a satisfactory manner based on performance and financial condition.

7. For brokers, dealers, and other third-party loan originators:

   (a) Assess the adequacy of the process used to qualify third-party loan originators.

   (b) Assess the adequacy of the reports and tracking mechanisms in place to monitor performance (e.g., volume of applications submitted, approved, and booked, quality, exceptions, and loan performance) and relationship profitability, including performance and profitability compared with projections.

   (c) Assess the adequacy of the process used to monitor compliance with the bank's lending policies.

   (d) Verify that management maintains a watch list for problematic originators and that actions taken (including termination of the relationship, if warranted) are appropriate and timely.

8. Assess the adequacy of the content, accuracy, and distribution of vendor management program reports.

9. Determine whether the bank has any loans to the third party and whether any conflicts of interest exist.

10. Determine whether any insiders have relationships with the third parties used by the bank and whether any potential conflicts of interest exist (e.g., insider has ownership interests, officer or board positions, or loans to the third party).

11. Determine whether the bank is involved in any significant third-party relationships where deficiencies in management expertise and/or controls result in the failure to adequately identify and manage the associated risk. If so, consult the EIC and the supervisory office and determine whether it is appropriate to require that the activity be suspended pending satisfactory corrective action.

12. Develop conclusions with respect to the extent of third-party involvement in retail lending activities and the effectiveness of management's third-party oversight and risk management processes. Clearly document all findings.

Debt Suspension and Cancellation

Objective: Assess the bank's debt suspension and cancellation programs, and determine the implications for income as well as credit quality, program performance, and level of compliance.

Note: These procedures should be completed if debt suspension and cancellation products have significantly penetrated the loan portfolio or shown substantial growth or plans for growth. The term "debt waiver" is used throughout the procedures below to describe these programs, regardless of whether a principal reduction is involved.

1. Determine whether the bank offers any type of debt suspension and cancellation products. If so, determine the retail credit products eligible for debt waiver programs (e.g., credit card, automobile, and home equity).

2. Determine program features and assess the adequacy of those features and whether they are accurately described in the marketing and the disclosures of terms and conditions provided to bank customers.

3. Determine whether marketing and promotional materials comply with 12 CFR 37.6(e).

4. Assess the adequacy of the policies, procedures, and practices in place for each debt waiver product or program. Test adherence to bank guidance and 12 CFR 37 by reviewing a sample of at least 30 approved and 30 denied claims.

5. Assess compliance with 12 CFR 37. Determine that the bank:

   (a) Does not extend credit or alter the terms or conditions of credit conditioned upon the customer entering into a debt cancellation contract or debt suspension agreement [12 CFR 37.3(a)].

   (b) Does not engage in any practice or use any advertisement that could mislead or otherwise cause a reasonable person to reach an erroneous belief with respect to information that must be disclosed [12 CFR 37.3(b)].

(c) Does not offer debt cancellation contracts or debt suspension agreements that give the bank the right to unilaterally modify the contract or agreement unless, (i) the modification is favorable to the consumer without additional charge, or (ii) the customer is notified of the proposed change and given a reasonable opportunity to cancel the contract without penalty before the change becomes effective [12 CFR 37.3(c)(1)].

(d) Does not offer debt cancellation contracts or debt suspension agreements that require a lump sum, single payment for the contract or agreement payable at the outset of the contract when the debt subject to the contract is a residential mortgage loan [12 CFR 37.3(c)(2)].

(e) Does not provide customers a no-refund debt cancellation contract or debt suspension agreement unless also offering a comparable product that provides for a refund of any unearned fees paid for the contract if the contract is terminated [12 CFR 37.4(a)].

(f) Obtains a customer's written acknowledgement to purchase a contract and written acknowledgement that the customer received the long form disclosures [12 CFR 37.7(a)].

(g) If the bank sells a contract over the telephone:
   – Maintains sufficient documentation to show that the customer received the short form disclosures and affirmatively elected to purchase a contract or agreement [12 CFR 37.7(b)(1)].

   – Mails the affirmative written election and written acknowledgement together with the long form disclosures to the customer within 3 business days after the telephone solicitation and maintains sufficient documentation to show it made reasonable efforts to obtain the documents from the customer [12 CFR 37.7(b)(2)].

   – Permits the customer to cancel the purchase of the contract or agreement without penalty within 30 days after the bank has mailed the long form disclosures to the customer [12 CFR 37.7(b)(3)].

(h) If a contact is solicited through written materials and the bank only provides the short form disclosures:
   – Mails the acknowledgement of receipt of disclosures, together with the long form disclosures, to the customer within 3 business

day, beginning on the first business day after the customer contracts the bank or otherwise responds to the solicitation [12 CFR 37.7(c)].

- Receives the customer's written acknowledgment of receipt of disclosures, unless the bank:

  i. Maintains sufficient documentation to show that it provided the acknowledgement of receipt of disclosures to the customer [12 CFR 37.7(c)(1)].

  ii. Maintains sufficient documentation to show it made reasonable efforts to obtain from the customer a written acknowledgement of receipt of the long form disclosures [12 CFR 37.7(c)(2)].

  iii. Permits the customer to cancel the purchase of the contract or agreement without penalty within 30 days after the bank has mailed the long form disclosures to the customer [12 CFR 37.7(c)(3)].

6. Select a sample of terminated debt cancellation contracts and debt suspension agreements to determine that the bank [12 CFR 37.4(a)]:

   (a) Refunded to the customer any unearned fees paid unless the contract provides otherwise [12 CFR 37.4(a)].

   (b) Calculates the amount of refund using a method at least as favorable to the customer as the actuarial method [12 CFR 37.4(b)].

7. Through discussions with lending officers and a review of the bank's training program, determine whether personnel provide and are trained to provide:

   (a) Short form disclosures orally at the time the bank first solicits the purchase of a contract [12 CFR 37.6(c)(1).

   (b) Long form disclosures in writing before the customer completes the purchase of the contract [12 CFR 37.6(c)(2)].

   (c) Long form disclosure in writing to the customer if the initial solicitation is in person [12 CFR 37.6(c)(2)].

   (d) Short form disclosures orally to the customer and mail long form disclosures, and a copy of the contract, if appropriate, to the customer within 3 business days after a customer solicits for the contract by telephone [12 CFR 37.6(c)(3)].

(e) Long form disclosures that are mailed to the customer on the first business day after a customer responds to a mail insert or "take one" application [12 CFR 37.6(c)(4)].

(f) Disclosures, if provided through electronic media, that are consistent with the Electronic Signatures in Global and national Commerce Act (15 USC 7001, *et seq.*) requirements [12 CFR 37.6(c)(5)].

8. Ensure that the bank complies with the disclosure requirements of 12 CFR 37, Debt Cancellation Contracts and Debt Suspension Agreements, by completing appendix E, "Debt Suspension Agreement and Debt Cancellation Contract Forms and Disclosure Worksheet."

9. Assess the quality of the MIS used to monitor and administer debt waiver programs. At a minimum, the bank's monthly debt waiver program reports should be sufficient to accurately ascertain:

(a) Enrollment volume and trends, including:
   - Number and account balances of accounts enrolled in the program.
   - Cancellation rate, segmented by customer versus bank closure.

(b) Application and activation volume and trends, including:
   - Average claim processing time, by type.
   - Benefit application, approval, decline, and fallout[19] rates.
   - Number and account balances of accounts in benefit status.
   - Average duration of benefit period by type and aging of active benefits (time to benefit exhaustion).
   - Delinquency status of accounts in active benefit status, by type.
   - Performance of accounts subsequent to benefit denial, fallout, and benefit exhaustion.

(c) Profitability, including:
   - Fee income generated.

---

[19] Fallout refers to failure to satisfactorily complete the debt waiver claim.

- Average annual percentage rate of enrolled and activated accounts.

- Costs, including retroactive adjustments, of active benefits, by type.

Note: If the bank securitizes, the above information should be broken down by receivable ownership (bank, trust, trust series, etc.), and aggregated for the managed portfolio overall. It should be used to evaluate program performance (current and trends, operational issues, etc.) and pricing, to establish adequate debt waiver interest and fee reserves, to set the amount of a trust's remittance (if any), and to analyze the allowance for loan losses.

10. Evaluate the quality and frequency of the debt waiver analyses performed:

   (a) Determine whether management analyzes the performance of accounts. Confirm that the analysis includes the performance of accounts, by type of benefit claimed (e.g., unemployment, medical), for accounts:
   - Denied claims.

   - Failing to complete claims after notifying the bank.

   - Subsequent to benefit expiration.

   (b) Determine whether the accounts in 10(a) perform differently than the rest of the respective portfolio. If so, ensure that the performance difference is appropriately incorporated into the allowance analysis.

   (c) Confirm the bank's analysis by reviewing a sample of accounts that came off benefits six months ago. Determine the current payment status of those accounts.

11. Determine whether the bank administers debt waiver programs in-house, or if they are outsourced to an affiliate or third party. If they are outsourced, review the governing contract, costs, and the controls in place to monitor performance.

12. Evaluate the accounting and profitability of the program:

(a) Determine the bank's accounting for debt waiver income and expenses.

(b) Ensure that the bank maintains an adequate reserve for claims benefits, if applicable.

(c) Assess the significance of debt waiver income to the bank's total income, and evaluate income sustainability in view of program volume, claims experience, and cancellation rates, at a minimum.

(d) If the program is offered for accounts that are securitized, determine the bank's responsibility for income sharing and claims payments and review the supporting accounting entries. Confirm that trust reimbursements are accurate and timely.

13. Complete appendix F, "Debt Suspension and Cancellation Product Information Worksheet," and retain a copy in the examination work papers.

14. Develop conclusions with respect to the bank's debt suspension and cancellation programs, including management and administration, and the implications for income as well as credit quality, program performance, and level of compliance.

Overdraft Programs

Objective: Ensure that credit risk related to overdrafts and overdraft programs is appropriately identified, managed, and reported, and that overdraft losses are recognized in a timely manner.

The following procedures should be used when the bank offers overdraft protection to customers through either:

- Traditional overdraft accommodations. A traditional overdraft accommodation is overdraft approval that is not communicated or marketed to the customer. Such accommodations may have a manual or an automated approval process.

- Marketed, advised-line overdraft protection. These programs inform customers that overdraft protection is a feature of their account and promote the use of the service. Institutions also inform consumers of their aggregate dollar limit of protection under the program. Coverage is automatic for customers who meet the institution's criteria.

If the bank administers an overdraft line of credit program where the line amount is based on the customer's ability to repay, refer to the other applicable supplemental procedures.

Note: Examiners should refer to OCC Interpretive Letter #914 and any subsequent OCC or FFIEC issuances for additional guidance on matters associated with overdraft products.

1. Determine the program(s) offered, and whether developed and administered internally or externally.

2. Review the characteristics of the program, including marketing practices, advertising, and customer disclosures.

3. Ascertain the criteria applied to qualify accounts for overdraft programs.

4. Determine how overdraft limits are established and the consistency of those limits for similar accounts.

5. Assess the adequacy of the bank's policies and procedures for overdrafts. Policies should address:

    *   Account eligibility, including minimum average balance required and minimum age of the account (number of months open) requirements.

    *   Criteria for paying overdraft or debit items.

    *   Overdraft limits for different types of deposit accounts, including dollar limits (amount of individual overdraft items and amount of cumulative overdraft items) and item limits (number of overdraft items).

    *   Guidelines on suspending overdraft privileges (usually when the customer has maintained an overdraft balance for "X" number of days).

    *   Exception approval and monitoring for overdraft limits and suspension guidelines.

- Criteria for canceling participation in the overdraft protection privileges, e.g., charge-off of an overdraft balance.

- Circumstances under which the overdraft protection, if a feature of the account, will be reactivated for accounts suspended or canceled.

- Criteria for establishing a payment plan for an overdraft, if the bank offers a payment plan option.

- Charge-off requirements and accounting treatment.

- Monitoring requirements.

6. If the bank uses a third-party overdraft protection program, assess the rationale behind management's decision to use a third-party provider, and ascertain whether the bank conducted an appropriate due diligence review. In addition, obtain a copy of the contract between the bank and provider and review the terms for adequacy. Specifically:

(a) Identify the role of the third party, including the services and support provided.

(b) Assess the reasonableness of the compensation agreement. If there are any income-sharing provisions, ensure that they are equitable and that the third-party provider shares in not only the benefits but also the costs (e.g., participates in credit losses, receives less income).

(c) Ensure that the contract includes reasonable right to cancel, and that termination clauses are not one-sided in the vendor's behalf.

(d) Ensure that the contract includes requirements for the regular and timely submission of the vendor's financial information and, if the vendor is involved with the ongoing administration or servicing of the product, that it provides the bank with the ability to audit the vendor at will.

Note: The risk posed to the bank by a third party's failure should be minimal if the bank merely purchases the product and uses it internally, assuming proper product implementation. However, the vendor's compliance or other guarantee is worthless if the vendor is not in business. Refer to "Third-Party Management" in "Supplemental Examination Procedures."

7. Review the bank's overdraft aging report and loss trends on its overdraft programs, and verify that management has established reasonable loss recognition guidelines. Overdrafts should generally be charged off within 60 days after the date the account first went into overdraft status. Direct the charge-off of stale items, as appropriate.

8. If the bank uses repayment plans to allow customers a longer term to pay off their overdraft, ensure that the accounts are not carried on the books beyond 60 days from the date of the overdraft. The accounts should be charged off and the subsequent plan payments treated as an allowance recovery. Direct the charge-off of stale items, as appropriate.

9. Verify that the amount provided to the allowance for overdrafts is appropriate based upon the loss history for this activity adjusted for any recent changes to underwriting and program terms.

10. Review the bank's Reports of Condition and Income to ensure that the bank is treating the asset and any losses appropriately. Specifically, confirm that:

   - The overdraft balances are treated as "Other Consumer Loans" on Schedule RC-C.

   - If the institution advises the customer of the available amount of overdraft protection, the unused amounts are reported as unused commitments on Schedule RC-L.

   - Principal losses and recoveries related to these accounts go through the Allowance for Loan and Lease Losses and are shown on Schedule RI-B.

   - Losses associated with fees are reversed against the income account in which originally recognized (if in the same accounting period) or charged against a loss allowance for uncollectible fees.[20]

11. Ascertain whether the bank has appropriate overdraft tracking and reporting systems and whether management regularly monitors and analyzes that information, including:

---

[20] Banks may charge off uncollected overdraft fees against the allowance for loan and lease losses if such fees are recorded with overdraft balances as loans and estimated credit losses on the fees are provided for in the allowance for loan and lease losses.

- Usage rate of the product as a percentage of eligible deposit accounts.

- Timeliness of overdraft repayment.

- Charges and fees per account and as a percentage of average balance.

- Losses as a percentage of overdrafts, by number of accounts and dollars.

12. In drawing conclusions about the bank's overdraft-related practices, document whether credit risk related to overdraft programs is appropriately identified, managed, and reported and whether overdraft losses are recognized in a timely manner.

Verification Procedures

Objective: Verify the authenticity of the bank's retail loans, and test the accuracy of records and adequacy of record keeping.

Note: Examiners normally will not need to do extensive verification. However, these procedures are appropriate when the bank has inadequate audit coverage of retail lending activities or when fraud or other irregularities are suspected.

1. Test the additions of the trial balances and the reconciliation of the trial balances to the general ledger. Include loan commitments and other contingent liabilities.

2. After selecting loans from the trial balance by using an appropriate sampling technique:

    (a) Prepare and mail confirmation forms to borrowers. (Loans serviced by other institutions, either whole loans or participations, are usually confirmed only with the servicing institution. Loans serviced for other institutions, either whole loans or participations, should be confirmed with the buying institution and the borrower. Confirmation forms should include borrower's name, loan number, the original amount, interest rate, current loan balance, borrowing base, and a brief description of the collateral).

    (b) After a reasonable time, mail second requests.

    (c) Follow up on any unanswered requests for verification or exceptions and resolve differences.

    (d) Examine notes for completeness and compare agree date, amount, and terms with trial balance.

    (e) In the event notes are not held at the bank, request confirmation by the holder.

    (f) Check to see that required officer approvals are on the note.

    (g) Check to see that note is signed, appears to be genuine, and is negotiable.

    (h) Compare collateral held in loan files with the description on the collateral register.

(i) If the loan is secured, determine that the proper collateral documentation is on file.

(j) Determine that advance rates and loan-to-values are reasonable and in line with bank policy.

(k) List all collateral discrepancies and investigate.

(l) Determine that any required insurance coverage is adequate and that the bank is named as loss payee.

3. Review disbursement ledgers and authorizations, and determine whether authorizations are signed in accordance with terms of the loan agreement.

4. Review accounts with accrued interest by:

(a) Reviewing and testing procedures for accounting for accrued interest and for handling adjustments.

(b) Scanning accrued interest for any unusual entries and following up on any unusual items by tracing them to initial and supporting records.

5. Using a list of nonaccruing loans, check loan accrual records to determine that interest income is not being recorded.

6. Obtain or prepare a schedule showing the monthly interest income amounts and the retail loan balance at each month end since the last examination, and:

(a) Calculate yield.

(b) Investigate any significant fluctuations or trends.

Appendix A: Transaction Testing

Overview

Examiners should perform testing procedures when the examiner-in-charge (EIC) determines that the OCC should verify a bank's compliance with its own policies and procedures or with regulatory policies, regulations, or laws. The EIC also institutes testing when the OCC should assess the bank's risk selection, the accuracy of its MIS, or the accuracy of its loan accounting and servicing. Testing procedures should usually be performed periodically on portfolios or targeted segments of the portfolios when there is elevated risk (e.g., subprime lending), an increase in delinquency and loss rates, new lines of business, new acquisition channels, rapid growth, or when loan review or audit is inadequate.

These procedures recommend judgmental sample sizes. The sample size and targeted portfolio segment may be modified to fit the circumstances. The sample selected should be sufficient in size to reach a supportable conclusion. Increase the sample size if questions arise and more evidence is needed to support the conclusion.

Examiners may want to consider using a statistical sampling process for reaching conclusions on an entire portfolio. Performing statistically valid transaction testing on portfolios of homogeneous retail accounts is extremely effective. The benefits of statistical sampling allow the examiner to quantify the results of transaction testing and state with a statistically valid confidence that the results are reliable. For additional information consult the "Sampling Methodologies" booklet of the *Comptroller's Handbook*.

Examiners conducting testing should be alert for potential discriminatory, unfair, deceptive abusive, and predatory lending practices (e.g., lending predominantly on the value of collateral rather than the borrower's ability to service the debt, making high-cost loans, providing misleading disclosures). If weaknesses are found or other concerns arise, consult the bank's EIC or compliance examiner.

Note: For additional information refer to the Comptroller's Handbook, "Fair Lending" booklet and OCC advisory letters 2002-3, "Guidance on Unfair or Deceptive Acts or Practices"; 2003-2, "Guidelines for National Banks to Guard Against Predatory and Abusive Lending Practices"; 2003-3, "Avoiding

Predatory and Abusive Lending Practices in Brokered and Purchased Loans";
2004-4, "Secured Credit Cards"; and 2004-10, "Credit Card Practices."

Suggested Transaction Testing Samples

Note: Sample sizes are suggestions only. The sample selected should be sufficient in size to reach a supportable conclusion. Expand the sample size if issues are found or more evidence is needed to support a conclusion.

Underwriting

Objective: Determine the quality of new loans and risk selection. Determine adherence to lending policy, underwriting standards, and pricing standards.

Sample size – 30	Loans/accounts booked in last 90 days. <ul><li>Include coverage of all significant product types.</li><li>Include all or target certain acquisition channels.</li><li>Include different price points.</li></ul>

Sample size – 10 from **each** significant third-party origination channel	Loans/accounts approved and booked in last 90 days. <ul><li>Include all significant third-party loan originators, including dealers and brokers.</li></ul>

Sample size – 30	Loans/accounts declined in last 90 days. <ul><li>Include coverage of all significant product types.</li><li>Include all or target certain acquisition channels.</li><li>Focus on applications not automatically denied if credit scoring is used.</li></ul>

Lending Policy Exceptions

Objective: Evaluate the quality and appropriateness of exceptions to lending policy.

Sample size – 30	Loan/accounts booked in last 90 days. <ul><li>Include all exception codes.</li><li>Include coverage of all significant product types.</li></ul>

	• Include loans with exceptions from all significant third-party loan originators, including dealers and brokers. • If exception coding is deficient, filter new loans for exceptions to loan-to-value, debt-to-income, credit history, etc. and select sample.

Overrides

Objective: Evaluate the quality and appropriateness of low-score overrides.

Sample size – 30	Loan/accounts booked in last 90 days. • Select loans that scored below cutoff and were approved. • Include all score override reason codes. • Include loans in all score bands below the cutoff.

Line Increases

Objective: Evaluate the change in credit risk and appropriateness of line increases.

Sample size – 30	Accounts with **automatic** line increases in last 180 days. • Select accounts from different products. • Select accounts from a full range of risk scores but with proportionately more accounts with lower scores. • Include accounts with line utilization greater than 75 percent. • Test for consistency with credit criteria. • Evaluate the size of the line increase relative to creditworthiness. • Consider how much credit risk is added to the portfolio.

Sample size – 30	Accounts with **manual** line increases in last 90 days. • Select accounts from different products. • Include accounts with line utilization greater than 75 percent. • Include accounts in over-limit status. • Test for consistency with credit criteria. • Evaluate the size of the line increase relative to creditworthiness.

| | • Consider how much credit risk is added to the portfolio. |

Over-limits

Objective: Evaluate the quality of accounts in over-limit status.

Sample size – 30	Accounts with balances that equal or exceed the assigned credit limit by a certain threshold (such as 20 percent or more) as of last statement cycle date. • Verify why accounts are over credit limits, and if there are any authorization, insufficient funds, or other issues involved. • Verify when over-credit-limit (OCL) fees are imposed, and if and when OCL fees are suspended. • Verify how the minimum payment is calculated. • Evaluate sample for accounts with negative amortization. • Determine length of time in OCL status.

Collection Activities

Objective: Evaluate appropriateness of collection activities and adherence to FFIEC Uniform Retail Credit Classification and Account Management Policy. *Note: Refer also to the checklist in appendix C.*

Re-ages

Sample size – 30	Open-end loans that received automated collection (non-customer service) re-ages in past three months. • Check compliance with FFIEC and bank policies.

Sample size – 30	Open-end loans that received manual collection (non-customer service) re-ages in the past three months. • Check compliance with FFIEC and bank policies.

Sample size - 30	Open-end loans that received customer service re-ages for more than one delinquency cycle (i.e., accounts greater than 30 days past due when re-aged) in the past three months. • Check compliance with FFIEC and bank policies.

Payment extensions and deferrals

Sample size - 30	Closed-end loans that received loan modifications in past three months that brought the loans to current status. <ul><li>Include loans that were two payments or more past due.</li><li>Check compliance with FFIEC and bank policies.</li></ul>

Rewrites and renewals

Sample size – 30	Closed-end loans that were rewritten and renewed in the past three months. <ul><li>Include loans that were 30 days or more past due.</li><li>Check compliance with FFIEC and bank policies.</li></ul>

Workout and forbearance programs

Sample size – 30 per program	Open-end loans in 1) external workout programs (CCCS) and 2) internal permanent workout programs. <ul><li>Include any program with payment amount, interest, or fee modification.</li><li>Verify how the minimum payment is calculated.</li><li>Select 50 percent of sample from accounts that entered program in last quarter.</li><li>Evaluate the reasonableness of forbearance programs, i.e. qualifying criteria, interest rate, payment amount, and repayment period.</li><li>Verify compliance with internal policies and procedures.</li><li>Determine length of time in temporary hardship program, if any.</li><li>Be alert to the movement of accounts from one program to another.</li></ul>

Sample size – 30 per program	Open-end loans in temporary hardship programs as of the examination date. <ul><li>Evaluate the reasonableness of forbearance programs, i.e. qualifying criteria, interest rate, payment amount, and repayment period.</li><li>Verify compliance with internal policies and procedures.</li><li>Verify how the minimum payment is calculated.</li><li>Be alert to the movement of accounts from one program</li></ul>

	to another.

Sample size – 30	Closed-end loans in 1) external workout programs (CCCS) and 2) internal workout programs.
	• Sample each product type, e.g., auto loans and home equity loans.
	• Include loans with interest rate and payment amount modifications.
	• Verify compliance with internal policies and procedures.
	• Evaluate the reasonableness of the program, i.e., qualifying criteria, terms, and collectibility.

Bankruptcy

Sample size 30 per loan type	Open-end and closed-end loans coded as bankrupt as of exam date.
	• Include borrowers in chapter 7 and chapter 13.
	• Assess compliance with FFIEC and bank policies.

Settlement

Sample size – 30	Open-end loans with settlement agreement in the past three months.
	• Verify compliance with internal policies and procedures.
	• Evaluate reasonableness of the repayment period.
	• Determine appropriateness of loan allowance and charge-offs.

Was past due, now current

Sample size – 30	Open-end loans that were 90 days or more past due as of three billing cycles ago, but current as of next billing cycle.
	• Include accounts with NSF check payments, if possible.
	• Check compliance with FFIEC and bank policies.
	• Determine how the loan returned to current status and its appropriateness.
	• Assess the accuracy of the loan accounting system and delinquency reporting.
	• Consider the impact of any irregularities on roll rates and loan loss method.

Sample size – 30	Closed-end loans that were 60 days or more past due as of three months ago, but current in the next month.
	• Check compliance with FFIEC and bank policies.
	• Determine how the loan returned to current status and its appropriateness.
	• Assess the accuracy of the loan accounting system and delinquency reporting.
	• Consider the impact of any irregularities on roll rates and loan loss method.

Exceptions to charge-off policy

Sample size – 30	Open-end loans more than 180 days past due as of exam date.
	• Include loans from each product type.
	• Verify compliance with FFIEC and bank policies.
	• Evaluate whether exceptions to FFIEC policy are appropriate.

Sample size – 30	Closed-end loans more than 120 days past due as of exam date.
	• Include loans from each product type.
	• Verify compliance with FFIEC and bank policies.
	• Evaluate whether exceptions to FFIEC policy are appropriate.

Charge-off post mortem

Sample size – 30	Recently charged-off loans.
	• Include loans from each product type.
	• Verify compliance with FFIEC and bank policies.
	• Review borrower, payment, and collection histories to determine whether actions taken pre-charge-off were reasonable or if the practices deferred loss recognition.
	• Evaluate whether exceptions to FFIEC policy are appropriate.

Fraud

Objective: Assess adherence to policy, determine propriety of practices, and determine timeliness of charge-off policies.

Sample size – 30	Open-end and closed-end loans identified as fraud, in part or total. • Determine whether accounts identified as fraud are being investigated. • Verify compliance with bank's policy and procedures, including what is considered fraud. • Determine whether fraud losses are properly identified as fraud losses rather than credit losses. • Determine compliance with charge-off time frames (within 90 days of discovery).

Debt Waiver

Objective: Verify how the product is managed.

Sample size – 30	Open-end and closed-end loans with debt cancellation contracts. • Include loans in both pending and activated status. • Determine whether the accounts are properly managed, i.e., activation process, accounting, re-aging, MIS, etc. • Verify compliance with bank's policy and procedures. • Verify compliance with 12 CFR 37.

Sample size – 30	Open-end and closed-end loans with debt suspension agreements. • Include loans in both pending and activated status. • Determine whether the accounts are properly managed, i.e., activation process, accounting, re-aging, MIS, etc. • Verify compliance with bank's policy and procedures. • Verify compliance with 12 CFR 37.

Minimum Payment

Objective: Verify how the minimum payment is computed.

Sample size – 30	Open-end loans for each product type.
	• Include accounts in over-limit status, in temporary hardship and workout programs, and with the credit protection feature.
	• Verify that product control file settings are consistent with bank's policy and appropriate.

Appendix B: General Request Letter

Please provide the following information for retail lending operations as of the close of business (DATE), unless otherwise indicated. Information in an electronic format is preferred. If submitting hard copies, please prominently mark any information/documentation that is to be returned to the bank.

Our intent is to request information that can be easily obtained. If you find that the information is not readily available or requires significant effort on your part to prepare, please contact us prior to compiling the data.

Please note that this list is not all-inclusive, and that we may request additional items during the course of our examination.

General

1. Summary of each retail credit product offered, and a brief description of characteristics and terms. Include descriptions of debt waiver products offered and merchant processing activities, if any. Also, include marketing or acquisition channels used (e.g., direct, Internet, mail, and third-party originators) where applicable.

2. Descriptions of any new or expanded products or marketing initiatives since the last examination and any upcoming plans.

3. Descriptions of any third-party loan generation (e.g., dealers and brokers) or servicing arrangements (e.g., collection agencies).

4. Descriptions of any retail portfolios acquired since the last examination, including due diligence reports.

Management and Supervision

Note: During the supervisory activity, examiners may request, review, and discuss individual manager's performance appraisals.

5. An organization chart(s) for the retail department's current structure. Include all key managers, the number of people in each department, and approved but unfilled positions.

---

6.   A list of primary contacts, including contact numbers.

7.   Job descriptions and brief resume/work experience summary for all key retail managers.

8.   A list of board and relevant senior management committees that provide retail area oversight, including a list of members and meeting schedules.

9.   Minutes of board and relevant senior management committees for most recent full year and year-to-date. Include any relevant retail-related reports provided to the committees.

10.   Most recent strategic plan with details of any assumptions used to prepare the plan. Include marketing plans and forecasts for retail products.

11.   Summaries of all incentive programs in effect in the retail department.

12.   A list of all key reports used by management to monitor the business, including frequency, distribution, and the person or unit responsible for report preparation.

Financial Performance

13.   Financial and profitability performance indicators for the retail department from the most recent year-end and for year-to-date. Copies of balance sheets and income statements from most recent year-end and for year-to date, including budget data for comparison purposes.

14.   Most recent budget with details of any assumptions used to prepare. Include any year-to-date budget variances and plan revisions as of the examination date.

15.   Profitability reports for each major lending product as of the examination date and the most recent year-end.

16.   A summary of any profitability models used and current rate and fee schedule for each retail product.

Control Systems (Risk Management, Loan Review, Quality Assurance, Audit)

17. Relevant reports issued by internal and external audit, quality assurance, compliance management, and loan review since the last examination. Include management's responses.

18. Policies and procedures for major functional areas, including underwriting, account management, collections, loan loss reserves, and quality assurance.

19. A chronology log of significant policy changes and other events relevant to the portfolio's performance.

20. Risk management reports and analyses used to monitor performance of the portfolio and individual products.

21. Loan volume reports by number and dollar amount for the entire portfolio and individual product.

22. Summary of monthly delinquency and net loss reports from the most recent year-end and for the year-to-date for the portfolio and individual products. Also provide any vintage analysis, dynamic delinquency, and loss analysis completed to monitor the portfolio. Include other credit performance analyses you feel are pertinent.

23. An overview of the scorecards used, if any, and summary of any changes planned.

24. Most recent model validation for each scorecard used.

25. Risk score distributions and migration trends.

26. Most recent loss forecasts.

27. If dealers, brokers, or other third-party originators are used, MIS used to monitor quality of applicants and credit performance of loans sourced from each third party used.

---

28. Description of controls (e.g., financial and audit requirements) and performance reports used to monitor the quality of service of third parties, as well as due diligence criteria used to select third parties for the retail activities.

Underwriting

29. Risk management reports used to monitor and analyze applicant quality and trends. Include application-tracking trend reports for the most recent year-end and year-to-date. Depending on the portfolio, information may include applications submitted, approved, booked, and denied, and underwriting criteria, such as credit grades, loan-to-value, credit score, and debt-to-income distributions/measures.

30. Reports used to track loan officer or underwriter productivity and compliance with policy.

31. Reports used to monitor underwriting policy exceptions and overrides. Please include any analyses of subsequent performance by type of exception.

Collections

32. An overview of how the bank achieves compliance with the FFIEC Uniform Retail Classification and Account Management Policy.

33. Volume and trends for loan extensions, including subsequent performance monitoring.

34. Volume and trends for re-age activities, if any, including subsequent performance monitoring.

35. Volume and trends of accounts in workout programs (e.g., CCCS) or other forbearance programs, including subsequent performance monitoring.

36. Problem loan list with credit risk classifications and criteria for assigning these risk classifications.

37. MIS used to monitor the volume and trends for repossession, foreclosures, and OREO (residential), as well as remarketing efforts. Include inventory aging and monthly trends for units, dollars, and deficiency loss trends.

38. Loan loss post mortem reviews from the most recent year-end and for year-to-date.

39. MIS reports used to measure the effectiveness and manage the collection area (e.g., roll rates, dollars collected, promises to pay).

40. MIS reports detailing the number and dollars of first payment defaults. If available, include monthly reports for the past 12 months.

Allowance for Loan Losses

41. Most recent allowance for loan and lease loss analysis for the retail portfolio. Include a complete description of the method and assumptions used.

Other Areas of Interest

42. Consumer complaint logs since the last examination.

43. Description of litigation, either filed or anticipated, associated with the bank's retail activities. Include expected costs or other implications.

44. If debt suspension or debt cancellation products are offered, MIS used to monitor product performance. Include information for product penetration, claims rates (approved and denied), reserve method and balances, and profitability.

Transaction Testing

Examiners will conduct transaction testing to verify compliance with the bank's policies and procedures; assess risk selection; determine accuracy of MIS; verify compliance with the applicable policies, laws, and regulations; or determine the accuracy of loan accounting and servicing.

45. Please provide electronic files for each major retail product that will allow an examiner to select a sample to conduct the testing. The file should be provided in a file compatible with the National Credit Tool (NCT) or an Excel worksheet that includes relevant loan information (e.g., account number, customer name, booking date, loan amount, payment information (current payment due, last payment date), loan term, interest rate, delinquency status, risk score, loan-to-value, and repayment capacity measure).

NOTES: If NCT is available, examiners are encouraged to use NCT sampling capabilities to assist in the transaction testing. Also, examiners may want to inform the bank of the types of transactional testing that may be performed. Examples are included below.

Areas To Be Tested
Loans approved in the last 60 days (since DATE). If credit scoring is used, provide two files, one for accounts not automatically approved and one for accounts automatically approved.
Loans approved in the last 60 days (since DATE) that would have been denied except for an override or exception to policy.
Loans that were 60 days or more past due as of (DATE), but current as of (DATE).
Loans extended, deferred, or rewritten in (MONTH).
Loans charged off in (MONTH).

Appendix C: Uniform Retail Credit Classification and Account Management Policy Checklist (RCCP Checklist)

Retail Credit Classification and Account Management Policy	Ref	Comments
Retail Credit Classification and Account Management Policy (Policy) Applicability: • Open- and closed-end credit extended to individuals for household, family, and other personal expenditures, includes consumer loans and credit cards. • Loans to individuals secured by their personal residence, including first mortgage, home equity, and home improvement loans.		
Note Regarding Minimum Policy Guidelines • The policy does not preclude examiners from classifying individual loans or entire portfolios regardless of delinquency status or criticizing account management practices that are deficient or improperly managed. If underwriting standards, risk management, or account management standards are weak and present unreasonable credit risk, deviation from the minimum classification guidelines outlined in the policy may be prudent. • Credit losses should be recognized when the bank becomes aware of the loss, but in no case should the charge-off exceed the time frames stated in the policy.		
Substandard Classification 1) Does the bank consider open- and closed-end retail loans 90 cumulative days past due *substandard*? 2) When a bank does not hold the senior mortgage on home equity loans, does it consider them substandard if they are 90 days or more past due, even if the loan-to-value is 60 percent or less (see note below)? 3) Are loans to borrowers in bankruptcy where the bank can clearly demonstrate that repayment is likely to occur appropriately classified substandard until the borrower re-establishes the ability and willingness to repay for a period of at least six months? *Note: The policy states that properly secured residential real estate loans with loan-to-value ratios of 60 percent or less may not need to be classified based solely on delinquency.*		

Retail Credit Classification and Account Management Policy	Ref	Comments
Loss Classification 1) Are unsecured closed-end retail loans charged off in the month they become 120 cumulative days past due? 2) Are secured closed-end retail loans secured by other than real estate collateral charged off in the month they become 120 cumulative days past due? 3) If the answer to #2 above is no, are these loans written down to the value of the collateral, less cost to sell, **if** repossession of collateral is assured and in process? 4) For open- and closed-end loans secured by residential real estate, is a current assessment of value made no later than when the account is 180 days past due? 5) For loans under #4 above, is any loan balance in excess of the value of the property, less cost to sell, charged off?		
Bankruptcy 1) Are loans in bankruptcy charged off within 60 days of receipt of notification of filing from the bankruptcy court or within the 120/180-day time frame (whichever is shorter)? 2) Are loans with collateral written down to the value of collateral, less cost to sell? 3) When a loan's balance is not charged off, does the bank classify it as substandard until the borrower re-establishes the ability and willingness to repay for a period of at least six months?		
Fraudulent Loans Are fraudulent loans classified loss and charged off within 90 days of discovery or within the 120/180-day time frame (whichever is shorter)?		
Deceased Accounts Are loans of deceased persons classified loss and charged off when the loss is determined or within the 120/180-day time frame (whichever is shorter)?		

Retail Credit Classification and Account Management Policy	Ref	Comments
Other Considerations for Classification Under what conditions would the bank not classify (substandard or loss) a loan in accordance with the policy? *Note: The policy permits nonclassification if the bank can document that the loan is well-secured and in the process of collection, such that collection will occur regardless of delinquency status.*		
Partial Payments 1) Does bank require that a payment be equivalent to 90% or greater of the contractual payment before counting the payment as a full payment? 2) As an alternative, does the bank aggregate payments and give credit for any partial payments received? 3) Are controls in place to prevent both methods above from being used simultaneously on the same credit?		
Re-aging, Extensions, Deferrals, Renewals, and Rewrites 1) Are the above type of activities only permitted when the action is based on a renewed willingness and ability to repay the loan? 2) Does documentation show that the bank communicated with the borrower, the borrower agreed to pay the loan in full, and the borrower has the ability to repay the loan? 3) Does MIS separately identify the number of accounts and dollar amount that have been re-aged, extended, deferred, renewed, or rewritten, including the number of times such action have been taken? 4) How does the bank monitor and track the volume and performance of loans that have been re-aged, extended, deferred, renewed, rewritten, or placed in a workout program? *Note: These requirements above do not apply to customer-service-originated extensions or program extensions (such as holiday skip-a-pay). Examples of how the bank would determine and document the borrower's willingness and*		

Retail Credit Classification and Account Management Policy	Ref	Comments

ability to repay could include such items as credit bureau score and data being obtained and reviewed, stated income being verified, and obtaining a "hardship" letter from the borrower.

Open-end Credit (Re-aging)

1) Is a reasonable written policy in place and adhered to?

2) To be considered for re-aging, does the account exhibit the following:

- The borrower has demonstrated a renewed willingness and ability to repay the loan?

- The account has existed for at least nine months?

- The borrower has made at least three consecutive minimum monthly payments or the equivalent cumulative amount?

- Does the bank prohibit the advancement of funds to make the minimum payment requirements?

- Does the bank limit the number of re-ages to no more than once within any 12-month period?

- Does the bank limit the frequency of re-ages to no more than twice within any five-year period?

- For over-limit accounts that the bank re-ages, does the bank prohibit new credit from being extended until the balance falls below the pre-delinquency credit limit?

3) Workout loan programs

- Does the bank require the receipt of at least three consecutive minimum monthly payments or the equivalent cumulative amount, as agreed upon under the workout or debt management program, prior to re-aging an account that enters a workout program (internal or third party)?

- Are re-ages for workout programs limited to once in a five-year period?

- At a minimum, does MIS track the principal reductions and charge-off history of loans in workout programs by type of program?

Retail Credit Classification and Account Management Policy	Ref	Comments

Closed-end Credit (standards, controls, and MIS required for each area)
 	
1) Has the bank adopted and adhered to explicit standards that control the use of extensions, deferrals, renewals, and rewrites?
 	
2) Do the standards include the following:
 	
   • The borrower has shown a renewed willingness and ability to repay the loan?
 	
   • The standards limit the number and frequency of extensions, deferrals, renewals, and rewrites?
 	
   • Are additional advances to finance unpaid interest and fees prohibited?
 	
3) At a minimum, does MIS track the subsequent principal reductions and charge-off history of loans that have been granted an extension, deferral, renewal or rewrite?		

Appendix D: Account Management and Loss Allowance Guidance Checklist

Account Management and Loss Allowance Guidance	Ref	Comments
Applicability of Guidance • This checklist should be completed for all institutions supervised by the OCC that offer credit card programs. The checklist should be used in conjunction with the related examination procedures. • Negative responses below may indicate that management is not complying with the guidance. In such cases, further review may be necessary to determine the appropriate corrective action.		
Credit Line Management 1) Does management test, analyze, and document line-assignment and line-increase criteria prior to broad implementation? 2) Does the bank offer customers multiple credit lines, such as bankcard plus store-specific private label cards and affinity relationship cards? If so, does the bank's management information systems aggregate related exposures and does management analyze performance prior to offering additional credit lines? Note: *Support for credit line management should include documentation and analysis of decision factors such as repayment history, risk scores, behavior scores, or other relevant criteria.*		
Over-limit Practices 1) Are policies and controls in place regarding over-limit authorizations? 2) Does management take appropriate actions to facilitate the timely repayment of the over-limit amounts (e.g., reduce or eliminate fees, raise the minimum payment, initiate workout programs)? 3) Does MIS enable management to identify, measure, manage, and control the unique risks associated with over-limit accounts? MIS should include: • Over-limit volume, segmented by severity. • Credit performance. • Duration of over-limit.		

Account Management and Loss Allowance Guidance	Ref	Comments
Minimum Payment and Negative Amortization 1) Do minimum payment requirements ensure that the principal balance will be amortized over a reasonable period of time, consistent with the risk profile of the borrower? 2) Do minimum payment requirements cover finance charges and recurring fees assessed during the billing cycle? *Note: Liberal repayment programs can result in negative amortization (where outstanding balances continue to build). Prolonged negative amortization, inappropriate fees, and other practices can inordinately compound or protract consumer debt, mask portfolio performance and quality, and raise safety and soundness concerns. These practices should be criticized.*		
Workout and Forbearance Practices **Repayment Period** 1) Do all workout programs provide for repayment terms that have borrowers repay their existing debt within 60 months? 2) What exceptions are allowed to the 60-month time frame? Are such exceptions clearly documented and supported by compelling evidence that less conservative terms and conditions are warranted? **Settlements** 3) For credit card accounts subject to settlement arrangements, are controls in place for setting the amount (dollar or percentage) to be forgiven and the requirement for the borrower to pay the remaining balance in either a lump-sum payment or over several months? 4) Is the amount of debt forgiven in a settlement arrangement classified loss and charged off immediately? If this is not done, does the bank treat such amounts forgiven in settlement arrangements as specific allowances? *Note: The creation of a specific allowance is reported as a charge-off in Schedule RI-B of the Reports of Income and Condition (call report).*		

Account Management and Loss Allowance Guidance	Ref	Comments
5) Upon receipt of the final settlement payment, are any deficiency balances charged off within 30 days? Note: *An open-end credit card account is a workout when its credit is no longer available and its balance owed is placed on a fixed (dollar or percentage) repayment schedule in accordance with modified, concessionary terms and conditions. Temporary hardship programs are not considered workout programs unless the program exceeds 12 months, including renewals.*		
Income Recognition and Loss Allowance Practices **Accrued Interest and Fees** 1) When determining appropriate loss allowances, does the bank evaluate the collectibility of accrued interest and fees on credit card accounts? 2) If the bank does not place credit card accounts on nonaccrual, does it alternatively provide loss allowances for uncollectible fees and finance charges? 3) For banks that securitize credit card receivables, does management ensure that the owned portion of accrued interest and fees, including related estimated losses, are accounted for separately from the retained interest in accrued interest and fees from securitized accounts? **Loan Loss Allowances** 4) Does management consider the loss inherent in *both* delinquent and nondelinquent loans? **Allowances for Over-limit Accounts** 5) Does the bank's allowance method address the additional risk associated with chronic over-limit accounts? Note: *To be able to identify these incremental losses, it is necessary for the bank to be able to track the payment requirements and performance on over-limit accounts.* **Allowances for Workout Programs** 6) Are accounts in workout programs segregated for performance measurement, impairment analysis, and monitoring purposes? (Multiple workout programs having different performance characteristics should be tracked separately.)		

Account Management and Loss Allowance Guidance	Ref	Comments
7) Is the allowance allocation on workout programs at least equal to the estimated loss in each program based on historical experience as adjusted for current conditions and trends? *Note: Adjustments should take into account changes in economic conditions, volume and mix, terms and conditions of each program, and collections.* **Recovery Practices** 8) Does the bank ensure that the total amount credited to the ALLL as recoveries on a loan is limited to the amount previously charged off against the ALLL on that loan?		
Policy Exceptions 1) Does the bank allow any exceptions to the FFIEC Uniform Retail Credit Classification and Account Management Policy? If so, what types of exceptions are allowed? 2) For exceptions granted, do the bank's policies and procedures identify the types of exceptions allowed and the circumstances for permitting them? 3) Is the performance of accounts granted exceptions to this policy tracked and monitored?		

Appendix E: Debt Suspension Agreement and Debt Cancellation Contract Forms and Disclosure Worksheet

Debt Suspension Agreement and Debt Cancellation Contract Forms and Disclosure Worksheet	Compliance Yes/No/NA	Comments
12 CFR 37.6(a) Content of short form disclosures **Appendix A to Part 37 — Short Form Disclosures**		
Product is optional Your purchase of [PRODUCT NAME] is optional. Whether or not you purchase [PRODUCT NAME] will not affect your application for credit or the terms of any existing credit agreement you have with the bank.		
Lump-sum payment of fee *Note: Applicable if a bank offers the option to pay the fee in a single payment. Prohibited when the debt subject to the contract is a residential mortgage loan.* You may choose to pay the fee in a single lump sum or in [monthly/quarterly] payments. Adding the lump sum of the fee to the amount you borrow will increase the cost of [PRODUCT NAME].		
Lump-sum payment of fee with no refund *Note: Applicable if a bank offers the option to pay the fee in a single payment for a no-refund debt cancellation contract. Prohibited when the debt subject to the contract is a residential mortgage loan.* You may choose [PRODUCT NAME] with or without a refund provision. Prices of refund and no-refund products are likely to differ.		
Refund of fee paid in lump sum *Note: Applicable when the customer pays the fee in a single payment and the fee is added to the amount borrowed. Prohibited when the debt subject to the contract is a residential mortgage loan.* *Either* (1) You may cancel [PRODUCT NAME] at any time and receive a refund; *or* (2) You may cancel [PRODUCT NAME] within _____ days and receive a full refund; *or* (3) If you cancel [PRODUCT NAME] you will not receive a refund.		

Debt Suspension Agreement and Debt Cancellation Contract Forms and Disclosure Worksheet	Compliance Yes/No/NA	Comments
Additional disclosures We will give you additional information before you are required to pay for [PRODUCT NAME]. *[If applicable:]* This information will include a copy of the contract containing the terms of [PRODUCT NAME].		
Eligibility requirements, conditions, and exclusions There are eligibility requirements, conditions, and exclusions that could prevent you from receiving benefits under [PRODUCT NAME]. *Either* (1) You should carefully read our additional information for a full explanation of the terms of [PRODUCT NAME] *or* (2) You should carefully read the contract for a full explanation of the terms of [PRODUCT NAME].		
12 CFR 37.6(b) Content of long form disclosures **Appendix B to Part 37 – Long Form Disclosures**		
Product is optional Your purchase of [PRODUCT NAME] is optional. Whether or not you purchase [PRODUCT NAME] will not affect your application for credit or the terms of any existing credit agreement you have with the bank.		
Explanation of debt suspension agreement *Note: Applicable if the contract has a debt suspension feature.* If [PRODUCT NAME] is activated, your duty to pay the loan principal and interest to the bank is only suspended. You must fully repay the loan after the period of suspension has expired. *[If applicable:]* This includes interest accumulated during the period of suspension.		
Amount of fee *For closed-end credit:* The total fee for [PRODUCT NAME] is ___. *For open-end credit, either* (1) The monthly fee for [PRODUCT NAME] is based on your account balance each month multiplied by the unit-cost, which is _____; *or* (2) The formula used to compute the fee is _____.		

Debt Suspension Agreement and Debt Cancellation Contract Forms and Disclosure Worksheet	Compliance Yes/No/NA	Comments
Lump-sum payment of fee Note: Applicable if a bank offers the option to pay the fee in a single payment. Prohibited when the debt subject to the contract is a residential mortgage loan. You may choose to pay the fee in a single lump sum or in [monthly/quarterly] payments. Adding the lump sum of the fee to the amount you borrow will increase the cost of [PRODUCT NAME].		
Lump-sum payment of fee with no refund Note: Applicable if a bank offers the option to pay the fee in a single payment for a no-refund DCC. Prohibited when the debt subject to the contract is a residential mortgage loan. You have the option to purchase [PRODUCT NAME] that includes a refund of the unearned portion of the fee if you terminate the contract or prepay the loan in full prior to the scheduled termination date. Prices of refund and no-refund products may differ.		
Refund of fee paid in lump sum Note: Applicable when the customer pays the fee in a single payment and the fee is added to the amount borrowed. Prohibited when the debt subject to the contract is a residential mortgage loan. Either (1) You may cancel [PRODUCT NAME] at any time and receive a refund; or (2) You may cancel [PRODUCT NAME] within ____ days and receive a full refund; or (3) If you cancel [PRODUCT NAME] you will not receive a refund.		
Use of card or credit line restricted Note: Applicable if the contract restricts use of card or credit line when customer activates protection. If [PRODUCT NAME] is activated, you will be unable to incur additional charges on the credit card or use the credit line.		

Debt Suspension Agreement and Debt Cancellation Contract Forms and Disclosure Worksheet	Compliance Yes/No/NA	Comments
Termination of product *Either* (1) You have no right to cancel [PRODUCT NAME]; *or* (2) You have the right to cancel [PRODUCT NAME] in the following circumstances: _____ . *And* *Either* (1) The bank has no right to cancel [PRODUCT NAME]; *or* (2)The bank has the right to cancel [PRODUCT NAME] in the following circumstances: _____ .		
Eligibility requirements, conditions, and exclusions There are eligibility requirements, conditions, and exclusions that could prevent you from receiving benefits under [PRODUCT NAME]. *Either* (1) The following is a summary of the eligibility requirements, conditions, and exclusions (the bank provides a summary of any eligibility requirements, conditions, and exclusions); *or* (2) You may find a complete explanation of the eligibility requirements, conditions, and exclusions in paragraphs _____ of the [PRODUCT NAME] agreement.		
12 CFR 37.6(d) Form of disclosures		
Disclosures must be readily understandable Disclosure must be conspicuous, simple, direct, readily understandable, and designed to call attention to the nature and significance of the information provided.		
Disclosures must be meaningful Disclosures must be presented in a manner that engages the customer's attention. Examples of methods that could call attention to the nature and significance of the information provided include: (i) A plain-language heading; (ii) A typeface and type size that are easy to read; (iii) Wide margins and ample line spacing; (iv) Boldface or italics for key words; and (v) Distinctive type style, and graphic devices, such as shading or sidebars, when the disclosures are combined with other information.		

Appendix F: Debt Suspension and Debt Cancellation Product Information Worksheet

Please answer the following questions for debt waiver programs overall, and complete the attached worksheet for each debt suspension/cancellation product offered. Indicate whether responses are based on discussions with management or on an examination, which included process review/verification.

For all debt suspension/cancellation products:

1.   Must the account be current to activate benefits? If not, are there delinquency limits with respect to benefit activation?

2.   If accounts are delinquent when benefits are approved, does the bank re-age the account to current, freeze it at the payment/delinquency status at the time the benefit event occurred, or freeze it at the delinquency status at the time of claim approval?

3.   At what delinquency status does the bank terminate coverage (e.g., cancel coverage/premium assessment at 90 days past due)?

4.   Does the bank stop premium assessments on accounts that are over-limit? If not, under what conditions does the bank "force" premium assessments on over-limit revolving accounts (i.e., book the premium even though it would be denied through the authorization process)?

5.   Does the bank satisfactorily track and analyze the subsequent performance of the following populations for at least twelve months:

   • Accounts denied claims?

   • Accounts that failed to complete claims?

   • Accounts following benefit expiration?

6.   If the default experience of the bank's retail loans is significantly worse than that of the population as a whole, is this information incorporated into the allowance analysis?

---

7. How does the bank compute the interest and fees associated with accounts in claims status? Specifically, since interest and fees for revolving accounts are generally suspended, how does the bank determine the associated interest and fees that would have been due on a month-to-month basis?

8. What is the bank's process for reserving for benefit claims? Is it sufficient to cover the total of existing approved claims, claims in process and reasonably expected to be approved, and an estimate of claims not yet submitted by accounts in which an event has occurred?

9. If participating loans are securitized and the bank is responsible for making payments to the trust, are the trust reimbursements accurate and made monthly?

10. Is the bank's MIS sufficient to generate the information needed to establish and maintain an adequate reserve?

11. Is the bank's MIS sufficient to monitor and manage the various debt suspension/cancellation products?

12. Is the bank's pricing based on a valid cost analysis (considering all associated costs)?

13. Does the bank periodically evaluate cost/benefit from the consumer's perspective? Is that analysis reasonable and reflected in the pricing?

14. Is flat rate pricing, if any, appropriate for low dollar loan amounts? Please explain.

15. How many written consumer complaints has the bank received regarding these products year-to-date and in the prior full year?

16. Is the bank planning to offer additional debt suspension/cancellation products or significant product (coverage, pricing, etc.) or marketing (channel, emphasis) changes? If so, please describe.

Product Name:
Offered Since:
Retail Credit Product(s) Covered:
Provider (bank, affiliate, third party):
Administrator (bank, affiliate, third party):
Responsible Bank Officer:

Benefits	Unemploy-ment	Disability	Leave of Absence	Death
Coverage – specify maximum number of months, N/A if not included, or yes/no for death:				
Cost (e.g., statement balance X .0069)				
Individual				
Joint				
Benefit				
Interest and Fees				
Principal				
Limits, if any (e.g., limited to # of months premiums paid prior to event)				
Offered to self-employed customers?				

Penetration:
    # of accounts paying premiums
    % of portfolio				

Claims rate* (# of claims submitted/# of accounts paying premiums), YTD and prior year				
Approval rate (# of claims approved/# of claims initiated), YTD and prior year				
Denial rate (# of claims denied/# of claims initiated), YTD and prior year				
Fallout rate (# of incomplete claims/# of claims initiated), YTD and prior year				

Bank income generated from premiums:
    Year-to-date amount (percent)
       of total business line revenue
       of total business line pre-tax net income
    Prior year (percent)
       of total business line revenue
       of total business line pre-tax net income				

Cancellation policy, including refund policy				
Cancellation rate (# of cancellations/# of accounts paying premiums pre-cancellation), YTD and prior year				

*Approval, denial, and fallout rates should balance to claims rate.

Attach a copy of the product terms and conditions.

Appendix G: Loss Forecasting Tools

Reliable forecasts of expected consumer charge-offs are critical for risk management, profitability, reserving, and capitalization. This supplement describes the three most common methods for forecasting techniques: roll rate, historical, and vintage analyses. Some banks use combinations of all three methods for different consumer portfolios or forecasting purposes.

Roll Rates

Roll and flow models are the most accurate short-term forecast technique. The name is derived from the practice of measuring the percentage of delinquent loans that migrate or "roll" from early delinquency to late stage delinquency buckets, or "flow" to charge-off. The most common method is the delinquency roll rate model, in which dollars outstanding are stratified by delinquency status, typically current, 30-59 days past due, 60-89 days past due, and so on through charge-off. The rates at which loans migrate or "roll" through delinquency levels are then used to project losses for the current portfolio. The table below describes the mechanics of using roll rate analysis to track the migration of balances over a four-month period (120-day charge-off period).

The Roll Rate Schematic

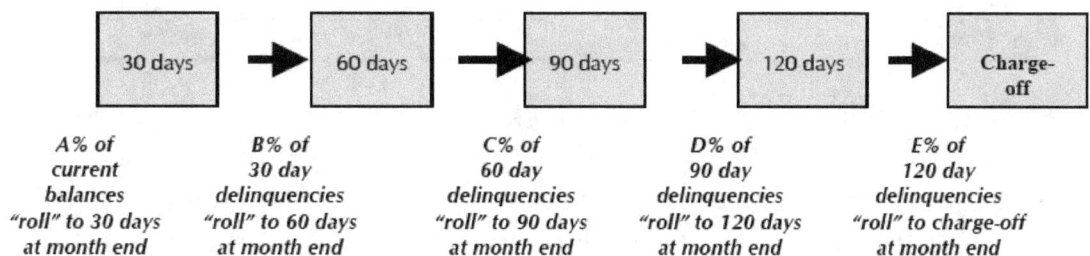

30 days	60 days	90 days	120 days	Charge-off
A% of current balances "roll" to 30 days at month end	B% of 30 day delinquencies "roll" to 60 days at month end	C% of 60 day delinquencies "roll" to 90 days at month end	D% of 90 day delinquencies "roll" to 120 days at month end	E% of 120 day delinquencies "roll" to charge-off at month end

Step 1: Calculate roll rates

Step 1 is to calculate the roll rates.[21] The computation begins with the $725 million in loans that were current in June 2000. From June 2000 to July

---

[21] The schematic and example above are simplified depictions of dollar flow to illustrate the basic concept of roll rates. In reality, some balances cure (return to current), remain in the same delinquency bucket, or improve to a less severe delinquency status by the end of a period. For ease of calculation, roll rate analysis assumes all dollars at the end of a period flow from the prior period bucket.

2000, $27 million in loans migrated from current to 30 days delinquent, which equates to a roll rate of 3.73 percent ($27 ÷ $725). From July 2000 to August 2000, $10.6 million rolled to the next delinquency bucket, representing a 39.26 percent roll rate ($10.6 ÷ $27). Continuing along the diagonal (shaded boxes), loss rates increase in the latter stages of delinquency. To smooth out some fluctuations in the data, management often averages roll rates by quarter before making current portfolio forecasts, and also compares quarterly roll rate results between quarters to analyze and adjust for seasonal effects.

Month	Current Balance	30 days	Roll Rate	60 days	Roll Rate	90 days	Roll Rate	120 days	Roll Rate
Jun 2000	$724.7	$26.1		$9.9		$6.7		$3.6	
July 2000	$762.0	$27.0	3.73%	$10.9	41.77%	$7.1	71.27%	$4.7	70.36%
Aug 2000	$788.6	$25.5	3.34%	$10.6	39.26%	$7.0	64.29%	$4.7	67.56%
Sep 2000	827.7	$29.4	3.73%	$12.1	47.82%	$7.9	74.88%	$5.5	78.74%
3Q avg.			3.60%		42.95%		70.15%		72.22%
Oct 2000	$844.6	$31.1	3.76%	$12.8	43.53%	$8.5	70.53%	$5.9	75.58%
Nov 2000	$896.3	$26.7	3.16%	$12.4	40.03%	$8.2	64.52%	$5.9	69.49%
Dec 2000	$987.3	$30.0	3.35%	$11.8	44.18%	$8.2	66.31%	$5.8	71.29%
4Q avg.			3.42%		42.58%		67.12%		72.12%
Loss Factors			.70%		20.61%		48.41%		72.12%

Step 2: Calculate loss factors by bucket.

Step 2 is to calculate loss factors for each bucket. To calculate the loss factor from the "current" bucket, multiply all average roll rates from the most recent quarterly average. In this example the fourth quarter average roll rates produce this factor: 3.42% x 42.58% x 67.12% x 72.12%, resulting in a 0.70 percent loss rate for loans in the current bucket. To determine the loss rate for the 30-day accounts, multiply the most recent quarterly averages for the 60, 90, and 120-day buckets, resulting in a loss factor of 20.61 percent. Applying the same method results in a loss factor of 48.41 percent for the 60-day bucket, and 72.12 percent for the 90-day bucket.

Step 3: Apply loss factors to the current portfolio.

Dec-31-00	Outstandings ($)	Loss Factor (%)	Loss Forecast ($)
Current days	987.4	.70	6.9
30	30.2	20.61	6.2
60	11.8	48.41	5.7
90	8.2	72.12	5.9
120	5.9	100	5.9
Totals	1,043.5	2.93	30.6

Step 3 is to forecast losses for the existing portfolio by applying the loss factors for each bucket (developed in step 2) to the current portfolio. In this example the portfolio's expected loss rate over the next four months is 2.93 percent.

The major advantage of roll rate analysis is its relative simplicity and considerable accuracy out to nine months. Portfolios are often segmented by product, customer type, or other relevant groupings to increase precision and accuracy. Roll rate reports are used extensively by collection managers to anticipate workload and staffing needs and to assess and adjust collection strategies.

The main limitation of roll rates is that the predictive power of delinquency roll rate declines after nine months. The delinquency focus causes forecasts to lag underlying changes in portfolio quality, especially in the relatively large current bucket. Portfolio quality changes occur because of factors such as underwriting and cutoff score adjustments, product mix changes, and shifts in economic conditions. Roll rate analysis may underestimate loss exposure when these factors cause portfolio quality to weaken. Finally, roll rate methodology assumes loans migrate through an orderly succession of delinquency stages before charge-off. In actuality, customers often migrate to charge-off status after sporadic payments or rush to that status by declaring bankruptcy.

Historical

Historical averaging is a rudimentary method for forecasting loss rates.

Management tracks historical charge-offs, adjusts for recent loss experience trends, and adds some qualitative recognition of current economic conditions or changes in portfolio mix. This method is highly judgmental and is used primarily by less sophisticated banks, or for stable, conservatively underwritten products. The most common of these products are residential mortgages when the collateral protection is conservative or the loans carry some sort of third-party guaranty or insurance.

The method is sometimes used for allowance purposes and monitoring general product or portfolio trends. The advantage is simplicity, and data needs are modest. Results can be reasonably accurate as long as underwriting standards remain relatively constant and economic or competitive conditions do not change markedly. The major limitation is that forecasts will lag underlying changes in portfolio quality if competitive or economic conditions change. The judgmental nature of the process also introduces potential bias by allowing forecasters to rely on longer run averages when conditions deteriorate and short-run trends at the earliest signs of recovery, either of which results in lower loss estimates. In addition, the method does not provide meaningful information on the effects of changes in product or customer mix, and it is difficult to apply any but the most basic stress tests.

Vintage

Vintage-based forecasting tracks delinquency and loss curves by time on books as different vintages or marketing campaigns season. The patterns or curves are predictive for future vintages, provided adjustments are made for changes in underwriting criteria, altered cutoffs, and economic conditions. The advantages of vintage-based forecasting are that its accuracy is usually better than roll rate forecasts for charge-offs beyond a one-year horizon, provided that the need for adjustments is readily observed. Management should adjust the future loss expectations when new vintages are observed to deviate markedly from past curves and trajectories, or if economic and market conditions change. The disadvantages of a vintage-based forecast are that it is more subjective and less accurate than roll rates for short-term forecasting and that it relies on the assumption that new vintages will perform similarly to older vintages.

Glossary

Acquirer, Acquiring Member, or Merchant Bank – A bank, financial institution, or other MasterCard or Visa member that maintains the merchant relationship and receives all credit card transactions. Sometimes referred to as the acquiring bank.

Adaptive Control System – Adaptive control systems are credit portfolio management systems designed to reduce credit losses and increase promotional opportunities. Adaptive control systems include software that allows management to develop and analyze various strategies that take into account the customer behavior and the economic environment. See Champion/Challenger Strategies.

Add-on – Additional service and credit products sold in connection with a credit account. Examples are travel clubs, disability insurance, credit life insurance, debt suspension insurance, debt cancellation insurance, and fraud alert programs.

Advance Rate – In financing consumer purchases, the amount that an institution advances in the form of a loan in relation to the value of the underlying collateral. For example, for new automobiles, the advance rate may be calculated based on the vehicle invoice or the manufacturer's suggested retail price (MSRP).

Adverse Selection – A disproportionately high response or acceptance rate to a marketing offer by high-risk customers in the targeted population. This situation generally occurs because the product or promotional design is flawed.

Affinity Program – A credit card program issued by a bank in conjunction with such organizations or collective groups as professional or trade groups, college alumnae associations, and retiree associations. The issuing bank generally compensates the sponsoring organization on some type of ongoing basis in return for access to its membership.

Agent Bank – A bank that, by agreement, participates in another bank's card program, usually by turning over its applicants for bank cards to the bank administering the card program and by acting as a depository for merchants.

Allowance for Loan and Lease Losses (Allowance) – A valuation reserve that is an estimate of uncollectible amounts (inherent losses), and that is used to reduce the book value of loans and leases to the amount that is expected to be collected. The allowance is established and maintained by charges against the bank's operating income, i.e., the provision expense.

Application Scoring – The use of a statistical model to objectively score credit applications and predict likely future performance.

Attrition – The closing of accounts. All retail credit loan products undergo attrition, but the term is most commonly applied to credit card accounts. "Prepayment" is used more often to describe attrition in closed-end retail credit products.

Balance Transfer – The transfer of an outstanding credit card balance from an account at one financial institution to an account at another institution. The receiving institution usually processes the transfer, but the consumer may effect the transaction by using convenience checks written on the receiving institution.

Bank Identification Number (BIN, VISA)/ Interbank Card Association (ICA, MasterCard) – A series of numbers used to identify the settling banks for acquiring and issuing credit card transactions. These identifiers are a component of the customer account number embossed on credit cards.

Bankcard Association – Visa and MasterCard are bankcard associations. In order to be a member of the associations and to offer their credit card services, the member must be a bank or thrift. The associations specifically define membership rights, privileges, and obligations.

Bankcards – General purpose credit cards bearing the MasterCard or VISA brands.

Broker – An individual or company that sources customers for loans and then places those loans with financial institutions for funding.

Buy Rate – The interest rate the bank charges for loans purchased through third-party dealers. Used in indirect lending.

Captive Finance Company – The financing arms of the automobile manufacturers such as Ford Motor Credit Company.

Cash Collateral Account – A credit enhancement common in asset-backed security structures. The cash collateral account is held in a segregated trust account, funded at the outset of the deal, and can be drawn on to cover shortfalls in interest, principal, or servicing expense for a particular series if the excess spread is reduced to zero.

CEBA Credit Card Bank – A special-purpose credit card bank chartered under the auspices of the Competitive Equality Banking Act (CEBA) of 1987. Such banks may engage in only consumer credit card lending and may accept deposits only to secure those accounts or in amounts greater than $100,000. These banks typically have a nonbank holding company parent and are often affiliated with a retailer. While they often issue private label cards, they may also issue general-purpose bankcards.

Champion/Challenger Strategy – A process employed to determine the most effective way of managing existing accounts. Usually driven by behavioral scores, the "champion" strategy is applied to the majority of the accounts, while various "challenger" strategies are applied to smaller portions of the portfolio. The results of the challenger strategies are compared against those of the champion to determine whether to install a new champion. Champion/challenger strategies are used extensively in the collection area for all types of retail loans, and for ongoing account management functions for open-end credit.

Chargeback – A dispute procedure initiated by the card issuer after the receipt of the initial presentment from the acquirer. The issuer may determine that, for a given reason, the transaction was presented in violation of the rules or procedures and is eligible to be returned to the acquirer for possible remedy.

Chronology Log – A chronological record of internal and external events relevant to the credit function.

Cobranded Card Program – A bankcard program issued in conjunction with another company, usually bearing the logo of the other company. The program is generally associated with some type of partner rebate or other value-added incentive to the customer.

Coincident – Refers to end-of-period delinquencies and losses in relation to total as of the same date. Distinguished from vintage, lagged, and other time series measures.

Consumer Credit Counseling Service (CCCS) – Nonprofit agencies that counsel overextended consumers, and funded by bank "fair share" contributions (a negotiated percentage of the consumer's payment to the bank). CCCS entities work with the consumers and their banks to develop a budget and a debt repayment plan. Banks generally offer concessions to customers in CCCS programs.

Consumer Reporting Agency – Any entity which, for monetary fees, dues, or on a cooperative nonprofit basis, regularly engages in whole or in part in the practice of assembling or evaluating consumer credit information or other information on consumers for the purpose of furnishing consumer reports to third parties, and which uses any means or facility of interstate commerce for the purpose of preparing or furnishing consumer reports.

Convenience User – A credit cardholder who pays the outstanding balance in full by each payment due date.

Corporate Card Program – Credit card programs offered to companies, small businesses, and government entities to facilitate company travel ("travel and entertainment" cards) and procurement. Ultimate liability varies by contract, but companies often provide some type of guarantee in the event of cardholder abuse or nonpayment.

Credit Bureau – A credit reporting agency that is a clearinghouse for information on the credit rating of individuals or businesses. The three largest credit bureaus in the United States are Equifax, Experian, and Trans Union.

Credit Report – Report from a credit bureau providing a customer's credit history. Credit reports are convenient and inexpensive with larger users paying lower rates. Mortgage lenders usually require more thorough and detailed credit reports. A merged credit report obtains files from the three major credit bureaus.

Credit Scoring – A statistical method for predicting the creditworthiness of applicants and existing customers.

Cross-Selling – The use of one product or service as a base for selling additional products and services.

Dealer – The retail outlet for automobile or manufactured housing sales. Dealers take loan applications from their customers and "shop" them to various financial institutions for approval and funding.

Dealer Reserve – Bank-controlled, dealer-specific deposit accounts used to accumulate the difference, when applicable, between the interest rate paid by borrowers on indirect installment loans and the rate at which the bank purchased the contracts from the dealers (see Buy Rate). Collected funds are released to the dealers per the terms of the dealer agreements.

Debt Burden Ratio – Measure of the consumer's ability to repay a debt. One common measure includes the debt-to-income (D/I) or debt service ratio, which measures monthly debt obligations against monthly income.

Debt Cancellation Contract – A loan term or contractual arrangement modifying loan terms under which a bank agrees to cancel all or part of a customer's obligation to repay an extension of credit from that bank upon the occurrence of a specified event.

Debt Service – A measure of a consumer's income in relation to committed debt payments.

Debt Suspension Agreement – A loan term or contractual arrangement modifying loan terms under which a bank agrees to suspend all or part of a customer's obligation to repay an extension of credit from that bank upon the occurrence of a specified event.

Deferral – Deferring a contractually due payment on a closed-end loan without affecting the other terms, including maturity, of the loan.

Extension – Extending monthly payment on a closed-end loan and rolling back the maturity by the number of months extended. The account is shown current upon granting the extension. If extension fees are assessed, they should be collected at the time of the extension and not added to the balance of the loan.

Fee Pyramiding – When fees result from the imposition of other fees. For example, when posting a late payment fee on a credit card account causes the account to exceed its credit limit and to incur an over-limit fee.

Five Cs of Credit – Term used to describe the evaluation criteria typically used in a judgmental credit decision: character, capacity, capital, collateral, and conditions.

Fixed Payment Programs (or "Cure" Programs) – Also described as workout programs, these include Consumer Credit Counseling Services (CCCS) and in-bank programs designed to help customers work through some type of temporary or permanent financial impairment. Cure programs typically involve a reduced payment for a specified period of time and may also include interest rate concessions.

High-Side Override – A denied loan that meets or exceeds the established credit score cutoff. To compute a bank's high-side override rate, divide the number of declines scoring at or above the cutoff score by the total number of applicants scoring at or above the cutoff.

Independent Sales Organization (ISO) – A third-party company that contracts with banks to acquire or service merchants.

Inherent Losses – The amount of loss that meets the conditions of Statement of Financial Accounting Standards (FAS) 5 for accrual of a loss contingency (i.e., a provision to the allowance). The term is synonymous with "estimated credit losses," which is used in the "Interagency Policy Statement on the Allowance for Loan and Lease Losses," issued on December 21, 1993.

Interchange – A portion of the discount fee (percentage of each transaction) paid by merchants on bankcard transactions. Interchange fees are established by the bankcard associations (MasterCard and VISA), based in part upon the type of merchant and the method of transmission from the merchant (i.e., online or off-line). The fee takes into account authorization costs, fraud and credit losses, and the average bank cost of funds.

Issuer – The institution (or agent) that issues a credit card to the cardholder, sometimes referred to as the issuing bank.

Lagged Analysis – Analysis that minimizes the effects of growth. Lagged analysis uses the current balance of the item of interest as the numerator (e.g., loans past due 30 days or more), and the outstanding balance of the portfolio being measured for some earlier time period as the denominator — generally six months or one year ago.

Low-Side Override – An approved loan that fails to meet the scoring criteria. To compute the low-side override rate, the number of approvals scoring below the cutoff score is divided by the total number of applicants scoring below the cutoff.

Loss Mitigation – Techniques of collecting loans used to reduce or eliminate the possible loss.

Managed Assets – Total balance sheet assets plus all off-book securitized assets.

Merchant Authorization – An issuing bank's approval of a credit card transaction in a specific amount. If a merchant complies with bankcard association rules in obtaining an authorization, usually by telephone or authorization terminal, payment to the merchant is guaranteed.

Negative Amortization – An increase in the capitalized loan balance that occurs when the loan payment is insufficient to cover the interest and fees due and payable for the payment period.

Open-To-Buy – The difference between the outstanding balance and the credit limit on credit card accounts. The total amount of committed and as yet unfunded credit available to borrowers is a contingent liability.

Pay-Ahead – The application of excess payment amounts to the next consecutive payment(s). As a result, the customer will not be required to make payments until the amount of the overage has been extinguished. For example, if a customer's automobile payment is $200 per month and the customer remits $600, the next payment will not be due until the third subsequent month. This practice is generally discouraged unless prearranged (to cover payments during vacations, for example). Excess payments should customarily be applied to the principal balance, thus reducing the number of total payments rather than interrupting the regular payment stream.

Payment Holiday (or Skip-A-Pay) – Programs giving the financial institution's most creditworthy customers the option of foregoing or skipping payments for a given month. Interest continues to accrue for the skipped time period. These programs are sometimes offered as frequently as twice a year, and usually coincide with summer vacations, August/September back-to-school shopping, or December holidays.

Penalty Pricing – Increased loan or line finance charge imposed when a borrower fails to pay as agreed, based on performance criteria in the loan or cardholder agreement.

Periodic Rate – The finance charge expressed as a percentage that is applied to the outstanding balance of an open-end loan for a specified period of time, usually monthly.

Point of Sale (POS) – Where a customer engages in a retail transaction.

Prescreen (or Preapprove) – To score or otherwise qualify a list of names or defined credit bureau population using credit bureau information with the intent of making a firm offer of credit to those passing the criteria.

Price Points – The price tiers which banks segment retail portfolios. Price points show both rates and outstandings in each tier. Especially important when teaser rates are offered, price points enable banks to model past, present, and future revenue and the impact of shifts that result from pricing strategies. Some banks identify three tiers, such as low-rate teasers, medium-rate standard products, and high-yield loans; credit card issuers might analyze up to 50 price points.

Private Label Credit Card – Credit cards issued for use at a single retailer.

Procurement Card Programs – Charge cards issued to facilitate corporate procurement. Balances on such cards are due in full each month or cycle.

Promise to Pay – A term used in collection departments to describe customers who have been contacted regarding their delinquent accounts and have committed to remitting a payment. Once the payment is received, it would be reported under "promises kept."

Re-age – Returning a delinquent, open-end account to current status without collecting the total amount of principal, interest, and fees that are contractually due.

Renewal – Underwriting a matured, closed-end loan generally at its outstanding principal amount and on similar terms.

Repossession – Seizure of collateral securing a loan in default.

Residual Value – Anticipated value or fair market value of an asset at the expiration of a lease.

Reissue – To issue new bankcards replacing those that have expired or will expire for qualified cardholder accounts.

Revolvers – Credit card customers who pay less than the full outstanding balance on their accounts each month (so that the account "revolves").

Rewrite – Underwriting an existing loan by significantly changing its terms, including payment amounts, interest rates, amortization schedules, or its final maturity.

Roll Rates – Roll rates measure the movement of accounts and balances from one payment status to another (e.g., percentage of accounts or dollars that were current last month rolling to 30 days past due this month).

Rollover – Carrying forward a portion of an outstanding balance on a credit card holder's account from month to month.

Secured Credit Card – Bankcards secured at least in part by deposit accounts held at the issuing bank or at a designated correspondent bank. The credit limit is often based on the amount of cash collateral provided.

Securitization – The process of creating an investment security backed by credit card receivables or loans.

Settlement – The process by which acquirers and issuers exchange financial data and value resulting from sales transactions, cash advances, merchandise credits, etc.

Spread Account – The most common form of securitization credit enhancement, a spread account carries reserves to absorb credit losses. The spread account generally equals two to three times the expected losses in the package of receivables/loans. It is initially "seeded" (funded) by the selling bank. These advances are usually expensed to achieve treatment as sales under regulatory accounting procedures (RAP). Excess servicing income is deposited into this account each month until it is fully funded and the seed money is repaid to the selling bank. The securitization trustee controls the account.

Stress Testing – Analysis that estimates the effect of economic changes or other changes on key performance measures (e.g., losses, delinquencies, and profitability). Key variables used in stress testing could include interest rates, score distributions, asset values, growth rates, and unemployment rates.

Sum-of-Cycle (SOC) Reporting – This type of reporting aggregates amounts based on their payment or billing cycle dates rather than opting for the point-in-time reporting used in end-of-month (EOM) reporting. The benefit of this type of reporting is the ability to compare performance of accounts with different cycle dates on equal terms — e.g., the total current vs. delinquent accounts as of the close of business on the payment due date.

Teaser or Introductory Rate – A temporary interest rate offered by open-end credit lenders to consumers as an incentive to open an account with their institutions. The teaser period generally lasts anywhere between three months and one year, and interest rates offered have been as low as 0 percent. Customers revert to the standard rate pricing after the introductory period.

Third-Party Vendors – Any third party that performs a function or provides a service on the bank's behalf. While generally associated with outsourcing, equipment and supply providers are also considered third-party vendors.

Trailing Documents – Refers to documents not yet received, in process, or otherwise incomplete in the real estate lending process.

Transactor – Credit card customers who pay their balances in full each month.

Travel and Entertainment Card Programs – Charge cards (balances due in full each month/cycle) issued to facilitate corporate travel and entertainment.

Vintage Analysis – Grouping loans by origination time period (e.g., quarter) for analysis purposes. Performance trends are tracked for each vintage and compared to other vintages for similar time on book.

References

Regulations

> 12 CFR 30 – Safety and Soundness Standards
> 12 CFR 34 – Real Estate Lending and Appraisals
> 12 CFR 37 – Debt Cancellation Contracts and Debt Suspension
>   Agreements

Comptroller's Handbook

> Allowance for Loan and Lease Losses
> Commercial Real Estate and Construction Lending
> Community Bank Supervision
> Credit Card Lending
> Fair Lending
> Internal and External Audits
> Internal Control
> Large Bank Supervision
> Loan Portfolio Management
> Merchant Processing
> Mortgage Banking
> Sampling Methodologies

Other OCC Publications

> An Examiner's Guide to Problem Bank Identification, Rehabilitation,
> and Resolution

OCC Issuances

> OCC Advisory Letter 1995-8, "Fair Lending (Credit Scoring-Age
>   Implications)"
> OCC Advisory Letter 1996-7, "Credit Card Preapproved Solicitations"
> OCC Advisory Letter 1997-8, "Allowance for Loan and Lease Losses"
> OCC Advisory Letter 2000-6, "Audit and Internal Controls"
> OCC Advisory Letter 2000-7, "Abusive Lending Practices"
> OCC Advisory Letter 2000-9, "Third-Party Risk"
> OCC Advisory Letter 2000-10, "Payday Lending"
> OCC Advisory Letter 2000-11, "Title Loan Programs"
> OCC Advisory Letter 2000-12, "Management of Outsourcing
>   Technology Services"

OCC Advisory Letter 2002-3, "Guidance on Unfair or Deceptive Acts or Practices"

OCC Advisory Letter 2003-2, "Guidelines for National Banks to Guard Against Predatory and Abusive Lending Practices"

OCC Advisory Letter 2003-3, "Avoiding Predatory and Abusive Lending Practices in Brokered and Purchased Loans"

OCC Advisory Letter 2003-7, "Guidelines for Real Estate Lending Policies"

OCC Advisory Letter 2003-9, "Independent Appraisal and Evaluation Functions"

OCC Advisory Letter 2004-4, "Secured Credit Cards"

OCC Advisory Letter 2004-10, "Credit Card Practices"

OCC Bulletin 1997-1, "Uniform Financial Institutions Rating System—Notice"

OCC Bulletin 1997-24, "Credit Scoring Models, Examiner Guidance"

OCC Bulletin 1999-10, "Interagency Guidance on Subprime Lending"

OCC Bulletin 1999-15, "Subprime Lending: Risks and Rewards"

OCC Bulletin 1999-38, "Interagency Guidelines for Real Estate Lending Policies"

OCC Bulletin 2000-3, "FFIEC Consumer Credit Reporting Practices"

OCC Bulletin 2000-16, "Risk Modeling, Model Validation"

OCC Bulletin 2000-20, "FFIEC Uniform Retail Credit Classification and Account Management Policy"

OCC Bulletin 2001-6, "Expanded Guidance for Subprime Lending Programs"

OCC Bulletin 2001-37, "Policy Statement on Allowance for Loan and Lease Losses Methodologies and Documentation for Banks and Savings Institutions"

OCC Bulletin 2001-47, "Third-Party Relationships, Risk Management Principles"

OCC Bulletin 2003-01, "Account Management and Loss Allowance Guidance"